Eccentric Gardens

Eccentric Gardens

JANE OWEN

Photographs by

ERIC CRICHTON

FOR JOHNNIE

Text copyright © 1990 by Jane Owen
Photographs copyright © 1990 by Eric Crichton

All rights reserved under International and Pan-American
Copyright Conventions

Published in the United States by Villard Books,
a division of Random House, Inc., New York
Villard Books is a registered trademark of Random House, Inc.

Originally published in Great Britain
by Pavilion Books Limited in 1990

Library of Congress Cataloging-in-Publication Data
Owen, Jane.
Eccentric gardens/by Jane Owen; with photographs by Eric
Crichton.
p.   cm.
ISBN 0–394–58447–3: $24.95
1. Gardens—Miscellanea.   2. Eccentrics and eccentricities—
—Miscellanea.   I. Crichton, Eric.   II. Title.
SB455.084   1991
635.9—dc20   90–50217
                                                         CIP

Manufactured in Italy

9 8 7 6 5 4 3 2 1

First American Edition

Excerpt from 'Little Gidding' in *Four Quartets*, copyright
1943 by T. S. Eliot and renewed 1971 by Esme Valerie Eliot
reprinted by permission of Faber and Faber Limited, London
and Harcourt Brace Jovanovich Inc., Orlando. Excerpt from
'In Memory of W. B. Yeates' in *Collected Poems* reprinted by
permission of Faber and Faber Limited, London and Random
House Inc., New York. Excerpt from 'Seeker of Truth' in
Complete Poems 1913–1962 by E. E. Cummings reprinted by
permission of Grafton Books Limited, London and Liveright
Publishing Corporation, New York.

Contents

Introduction

Eccentric Gardens celebrates the marriage of two glorious English traditions: gardens and eccentricity. By their nature gardeners are a dedicated, obsessional breed, and as the obsession grows, the gardener sometimes moves into an outdoor world of his or her own, blissfully careless of fads, fancies and traditions of garden design. The results are as curious and charming as the people who make them, and a cosy garden or an elegant one becomes instead a theatre for quirky jokes and tricks, for visual and horticultural oddities.

By the nature of the subject, eccentric gardens cannot be slotted into neat historical or sociological categories. They are not even green-fingered rebellions against traditional garden design. The gardens are one-offs: idiosyncratic eruptions of spirit and style and they come in every size, shape and situation from grand country estates to humbler backyards. Eccentricity, thank heaven, knows no bounds, so you can find an eccentric garden practically anywhere, as long as you are willing to look. The stories about how they evolve are as odd as the gardens themselves, because the gardens are created by people who want to make their own mark on the landscape in their own way. Unlike most of us, who soak up inspiration from lushly illustrated books, magazines and catalogues or from fireside reveries about summer afternoons at such blissful gardens as Gertrude Jekyll's Hestercombe or the National Trust garden at Tintinhull tended by Penelope Hobhouse, most of the gardens in this book are slaves to no other style than their own.

Most gardeners are dotty in a dedicated kind of way; they devote themselves to backbreaking, wet, muddy work, being scratched and frozen to death for one part of the year and then roasted alive for another, all for the sake of the few heady months when a garden bedazzles (so long as mildew and rust haven't taken control, the greenfly and blackfly plague isn't too severe and no water shortage is declared). Anyone who is prepared to undergo such extremes has to be strangely single-minded and astonishingly stoical in the face of adversity. Perhaps the solitary nature of the work – broken occasionally by chats with the *Rheum palmatum* 'Atrosanguineum', or by an ecstatic meeting with a fellow auricula lover to swap intelligence and plants – drives gardeners into mellow madness.

We are green-fingered and green-veined. When we can't make gardens, we fantasize about them instead. Some like Wemmick's in *Great Expectations*, are realized only between the covers of a book. What an astonishing garden it was, with a drawbridge between the street outside and the wooden cottage in Walworth where Wemmick lived, a free-standing gun emplacement from which a shot was fired at nine o'clock in the evening (Greenwich Mean Time), and a collection of pigs, fowl and rabbits squeezed in. Pip describes his tour of the Wemmick garden: '. . . he conducted me to a bower about a dozen yards off, but which was approached by such ingenious twists of path that it took quite a long time to get at . . . Our punch was cooling in an ornamental lake on whose margin the bower was raised. This piece of water (with an island in the middle which might have been the salad for supper) was of circular form, and he constructed a fountain in it, which, when you set a little mill going and took a cork out of a pipe, played to that powerful extent that it made the back of my hand quite wet.'

Then there are the chatty flowers which meet Alice in *Through the Looking Glass*.

'"Aren't you sometimes frightened at being planted out here with nobody to take care of you?" asked Alice.

"There's a tree in the middle," said the Rose. "What else is it good for?"

"But what could it do if any danger came?" Alice asked.

"It could bark," said the Rose.

"It says 'Bough-wough!'" cried a Daisy: "that's why its branches are called boughs!"'

I happen to enjoy the unexpected in gardens, although some may find it vulgar. R. Clipston Sturgis, for one, would not have enjoyed the gardens included in this book. He was writing at the beginning of the century, and the following damnatory passage is about Friar Park, a contemporary garden made by Sir Frank Crisp: 'The making of surprise, such as the sudden revealing of unsuspected features in the garden scene, must always be considered as evidence of debased taste, the prostituting of a beautiful art, for the sake of securing a momentary exclamation of

astonishment.' This book is simply a tour around some curious gardens and landscapes, occasionally seen through the illuminating eyes of the people who dreamed up and realized their landscape fantasies.

In the following chapters I have taken a deliberately narrow view and have focused exclusively on eccentric English gardens: the English have a particular claim on eccentricity which seems fundamental to their natural personality, having had years of civilization in which to develop their oddities. A study of gardening eccentricity could, I thought, justifiably begin and end there. But I have met crazy Texans and quirky New Englanders, and know that an eccentric garden can leap across an ocean as readily as anything else. I know the English and their gardens best. Call it laziness or xenophobia, but I have decided to limit my eccentric garden survey to England, though with some regrets.

In so doing I have embraced every kind of garden old and new, well known and ignored. Few of them can be adequately analysed and explained, precisely because they are unlike anything that has gone before. For the sake of some

semblance of order, each chapter heading roughly covers a theme uniting a genre of eccentric gardens and including some background from more famous, mainstream gardens to set them in context. At the back of the book you will find a gazetteer, a region-by-region guide explaining which gardens are open to the public and which are not. Visit these gardens with an open mind, in the knowledge that quantities of love and care, as well as hard work, have gone into each odd landscape.

Gardeners are the key to understanding the gardens included in this book, and so wherever possible I have left it to them to explain how the garden came about and why they created it. The answers are as disparate as the gardens themselves: some refuse to see anything unusual about half-drowned statuary of wire-mounted plastic goldfish flying between two ponds, others say they just like a laugh. For the gardens where records about their making have disappeared with their makers, there is nothing to do but wonder at the fantastic landscape left behind.

Jane Owen

Carswell Marsh 1989

The Surreal Plot

Ivan and Angie Hicks are nowhere to be found. They are not in their house, where a lump of sky, painted on canvas, has fallen above their front door. At first glance they do not appear to be in the garden either, until a shout from the sky reveals them, high above us, growing out of the top of a twenty-foot yew. It is an old yew to one side of the Hicks's house, and it has had its top carved out to make a nest for Ivan and Angie, with a secret back staircase of ladders which leads up on to the platform of wood and carpet where they can curl up together. Now they are in there with their children.

To walk into the Hicks's garden is to enter a Magritte painting improvised with a touch of Dali. It is a small plot in the middle of a Sussex valley, no more than half an acre at most, and it is packed with both rare and common trees and plants. Curious ornaments abound, and everything is contained within thick, high boundary hedging.

The garden is a remarkable creation especially for someone with no early background in the arts or in gardens. Ivan Hicks is a south London boy, one of eight children, from a family where gardens and surrealism played no part. He was bad and bored at school, and did not bother to go in much. But unlike his fellow truant scholars, who terrorized old ladies and became street sharp in the rough-tough city, Ivan Hicks would spend his dinner money on fares to the Tate Gallery and the Victoria and Albert Museum and Library. No wonder he is so thin and knowledgeable.

And then trees got into his system, so he went to Merrist Wood college where he read arboriculture, and then he replied to an advertisement placed by Edward James, the millionaire eccentric. Ivan became head gardener to Edward James, whose fanciful whims were to take Ivan to Mexico and Italy as well as Sussex to bring to life surreal gardens. With Edward James, Ivan Hicks was able to indulge his fantasies, including his childhood love of Rupert Bear, whose magical world was filled with plants and butterflies and animals. Together James and Hicks adventured in magic, fantasy and landscapes.

Today Ivan Hicks is garden manager of the late Edward James's estate at West Dean, where he is in charge of a team of gardeners, one arboretum and thirty acres of garden and a flock of peacocks (once there were three hundred but they have been dying off since James himself died in 1984 aged seventy-seven). Edward James is buried in the sweet earth that once nurtured his horticultural dreams, but his unofficial memorial is the Hicks's own garden, just beyond the crinkle-crankle walls of West Dean's old kitchen garden, now a nursery open to the public. Unlike the

LOBSTER AT REST IN
THE HICKS'S GARDEN

ABOVE IVAN HICKS AND HIS
DAUGHTERS, ALICE AND
LYDIA, JOIN THE SKY LADY
AND THE GREEN MAN IN THE
HICKS'S SUSSEX GARDEN

RIGHT THE SKY LADY AND THE
GREEN MAN

stately estate gardens at West Dean, Ivan Hicks's garden moves and changes hour by hour in both its hard and soft landscaping. Beside the huge old yew, to one side of the lawn, a plastic lobster is sitting on a chair painted with a skyscape of scudding clouds; minutes later the lobster apparently moves to the top of a free-standing pillar on the other side of the lawn. A lady's bust, cloud-painted too, moves from her perch on a huge coiled iron spring to the top of another pillar, which is also painted with a skyscape.

Spring may no longer be here, but to make up for it metal springs, spirals of steel, appear everywhere: on the lawn at the centre of the garden; beside the pond; in bowers tucked into the edges of the garden, and in flower beds where box edges try to discipline an abundance of roses, juniper, honeysuckle, aquilegia, verbascum, sweet rocket, foxgloves, rhus, rubus and nicotiana. As the day progresses, an iron sun circles the emerald green lawn. Ivan Hicks explains this by saying that because a garden grows and evolves it is only proper that the pattern of garden decorations should alter and grow and die with the vegetation.

Pushing out of the lawn in front of the house is The Mount, which could be considered to be very seventeenth-century except for the fact that it is tiny, and a wisp of a path coils down it to join a spiral of lawnmower track which ripples outwards across the lawn. Sometimes a great stack of empty beehives, representing a tower, clambers towards the sky from the top of The Mount. Sometimes one of the cloud-painted pillars stands on top instead, and sometimes a small pediment is placed there, on top of one of the iron springs, so that at night, as you stare out of the Hicks's front room, the light catches the white of the pediment and it appears eerily suspended, without any visible means of support. Once, when the beehive stack (or tower) with a ladder leaning against it stood on The Mount, some of the Hicks's friends arrived with a six-foot snake, a boa constrictor in need of a little Sussex air. So the snake obligingly curled in and out of the ladder while the Hicks and their friends played snakes and ladders.

Two shoe lasts tiptoe across the lawn, one painted with country scenes, the other with a twilit skyscape. Hiding behind a foxglove tree (*Paulownia fargessii*) is a small, ornate summerhouse built from an old window frame which had been thrown out of West Dean House; this Ivan Hicks calls the Crystal Palace. All the garden decoration is made from oddments and throw-outs lovingly revived and mingled together and painted. Acrylic paint, emulsion mixes and other people's rubbish are the nuts and bolts of this garden. Much of the planting comes from cuttings or from self-sown seeds blown there by the wind or is brought in by a bird or by some visiting animal or gardener.

New personalities are constantly arriving to inhabit the Hicks's garden. Two mannequins arrived looking for, and finding, shelter. The male has been named the 'Green Man', the female the 'Sky Lady'. He has been painted in fantastic landscape scenes, with a folly on his breast, a mount curling around his tummy button, and his neck and head a skyscape. She is cloud-painted, and hides demurely in the flower bed beneath the cherry tree.

Around the corner of the house, just beyond the yew containing Ivan's platform watchtower, there is the place he has named 'the magic garden', although it is unclear why it should be considered more magic than the rest. There is a pond with mirrors plunged into it, clematis, a fernery, a 'Kiftsgate' rose which rampages freely, hostas, a cloud-painted globe floating in the pond and much more strange statuary. Prisms from an old chandelier dangle from trees, throwing rainbows about the garden, and a totally useless chair – an elegant thin metal frame with no way of resting even the slimmest bottom – stands beneath a sunshade through whose frame the sunlight pours unhindered. Everywhere you look in the Hicks's garden there is a pleasing or beautiful scene, but each scene forces the observer to double take: the first look shows beauty, the second strangeness.

When Ivan Hicks moved into the gardener's cottage at West Dean, in the 1970s, he brought with him a tulip tree which was planted in the vegetable plot, so deciding the fate of that part of the garden. The tulip tree was joined in one of the large, curving beds around the front lawn by Serbian spruce, *Magnolia grandiflora*, and a *Prunus* 'Shirotae' ('In spring it looks like a cumulus cloud floating around the lawn,' says Ivan Hicks). He planted them and now wishes he had done more planting, because if he had grown plenty of box and yew all those years ago he would have more mature specimens with which to topiarize to his heart's content: boxes of box, spirals, erect phallic shapes and who knows what. But when he was Edward James's gardener there wasn't much time for his own garden: instead there were years of adventure, mostly garden-linked, which must to some degree be an influence behind this strange garden. There were adventures in bright orange Volvos with Edward James, trying to smuggle three peacocks, three golden pheasant and one silver pheasant across the border into Eire from Northern Ireland as a thankyou present to one of the Guinesses, with whom he had been staying.

They got there in the end, although, sadly, the bird life presents had to stay in Northern Ireland. Still, it prepared Ivan Hicks for further adventures,

ABOVE CRYSTAL PALACE WAS
MADE FROM CAST-OFF
WINDOW FRAMES

RIGHT ADMIRE IVAN'S
PLANTING OR BUST: A CLOUD-
PAINTED COLUMN HELPS

16

plant-oriented this time. Edward James announced that he wanted magnolias, giant lilies, roses, ferns and orchids to flower in his Mexican retreat, the Dali-inspired landscape in Xilitla, where he built great stairway sweeps, columns and free-standing Gothic-style casements in the middle of the jungle. Ivan Hicks was summoned from Sussex to the jungle with roots, seeds and bulbs secreted about his person. Few of the roses and magnolias took: it was too humid and shady. But the lilies took to life in the jungle with great ease, and so Ivan Hicks had to learn how to smuggle the corms of what were to become one of his master's favourite plants: *Cardiocrinum giganteum*, those huge and splendid lily-like plants with long greeny white downward staring trumpets which can smell like concentrated nicotiana on a summer's evening.

In Italy too, where Edward James was building a house as well as a garden, subterfuge was called for. Contrary as always, Edward James refused to have any palms in his Italian garden. They were too elitist, too Riviera. But he was keen on bamboos . . . and the only decent supply of the stuff came from a bamboo nursery in the south of France. Once more Ivan Hicks was forced to become a smuggler, hauling consignments of bamboo across the Franco Italian border in an Alfa Romeo sports car (of course).

The plans for all these adventures were laid out in

long rambling letters to Ivan Hicks from Edward James, who spent a large portion of the year outside the country as a tax exile, leaving Ivan Hicks to manage West Dean gardens. Their letters became works of art in their own right, wonderfully decorated and embellished. Even the envelopes were painted with skyscapes and comments and poems. And they had to be sent through the post, the stamp postmarked like any ordinary letter, in order to complete the work of art properly. A card from Milan dated 6 May 1984 is decorated with an Edward James painting of a man/tree crucifixion scene growing through the centre of the message: 'My Dear Ivan, do you remember that I have always planned a pool in the Monkton arboretum shaped like an enormous violoncello? We must start on this next, no I mean THIS July … or it will never be done ……………??' The card is an exception. Most of the communications from Edward James to Ivan Hicks ramble on for twenty or thirty pages at a time, mixing gossip about princely house parties with instructions about plants and trees, descriptions of hard and soft landscaping designs in the places he has visited and grumbles about the accessibility or otherwise of specialized composts.

Then there was Monkton House, Edward James's home and a refuge of eccentricity tucked deep into the most secret part of the West Dean estate. Despite a fight from the Thirties Society and others, the extra-ordinary contents of Monkton – a 'lips' sofa by Salvador Dali, a corridor carpet woven with paw marks, and many more oddities – were sold off after Edward James's death. It was in the Monkton House garden more than anywhere that Edward James and Ivan Hicks collaborated to create a crazy landscape. As you came upon Monkton along bumpy, unmetal-led roads you would sometimes be greeted by a boom of classical music coming from loudspeakers attached to the chimneys. Here Edward James, having refused to plant palm trees in his Italian garden because they were sometimes regarded as status symbols, had wooden palm trees made to stand outside his windows.

Gradually Ivan Hicks decided that he would stay and work at West Dean rather than moving on and playing the itinerant, as he had for some of his earlier life. So he started work on his own garden in the occasional chunks of spare time left by Edward James's demands. While he was in Britain, James took an increasing interest in Ivan's garden, asking him to plant favourites like the roses 'Ville de Bruxelles' and 'Gypsy Boy' (or 'Zigeunerknabe') and encouraging extravagance in design and exec-ution. Even Ivan Hicks's house, the gardener's cot-tage, reflects the close relationship between the gardener and his boss. On one wall behind the door hangs a copy of Magritte's picture of Edward James: the back of his head. The floor beside the door is sky – well, painted sky.

But the garden came first. And so did Ivan Hicks's love of trees. He planted a giant redwood which will one day presumably tower over the surrounding hills like a Colossus in the gentle Sussex valley. He planted a metasequoia and American dogwood, and the tiny-flowered delicate pink rose, 'The Fairy'. He made low arches under which you have to bend as you come into the garden and as you enter the magic garden. These remind you to show humility in the garden in much the same way as the Japanese encourage humility in their gardens by adding low arches around the perimeter. Ivan Hicks's arches are magnificent arches of reinforcing rod like the rods you see being built into the centre of concrete motorway pillars – but all wound round with clematis and roses.

In the early 1980s Ivan Hicks built The Mount outside his front door. It is round and fecund, like a miniature Silbury Hill, as if the earth itself were pregnant, and he regarded it as one of the symbols of the poetic form of the earth mother, the 'White Goddess'. Soon after The Mount arrived Ivan met Angie; they fell in love and started a family. Angie has had a great influence on the garden. She became Ivan Hicks's muse and helper – as he says, 'a lover of me and of the garden'. She also did practical things like the weeding. Like the rest of the garden The Mount evolved and changed. 'It has gradually become formalized into the potent spiral hill surrounded by concentric circles – or rather eccentric circles. The hill is off-centre too. Edward James, who was often described as an eccentric, said, 'Well, as that means I am off-centre, I certainly am.'

OFF-CENTRE
ORNAMENT

'I suppose we are creating – in a bizarre way – our own Garden of Eden, or Paradise Garden with symbolic, emblematic, romantic, surrealist and even dada associations. Many of the objects and features in the garden are things we have found and given new identity. This all sounds a bit pedantic but it should be taken tongue in cheek. We have a lot of fun, and our little girls love it. We let our imaginations flow.'

Although Edward James was interested in Ivan Hicks's garden, he had not the time to contribute much, and anyway, with Ivan's fertile imagination there was no need. But in Edward James's unpublished novel *The Gardener Who Saw God*, which is set at West Dean, there is some inkling of his surreal garden ideal and of the fellow spirit he recognized in Ivan Hicks. The garden he describes is, not surprisingly, like the scenes and landscapes from Dali and Magritte paintings, and yet despite Edward James's vivid descriptions of fantastic landscapes at West Dean, he executed very few of them. Instead, Ivan Hicks has done so in his own garden, albeit on a small scale and on a shoestring.

However, the millionaire patron of the arts did manage one odd scheme in the grounds of West Dean. Beech trees were among Edward James's favourites, and when two old beeches died in 1970 he had them chopped to twelve feet high rather than pulling them out completely. He then coated them in fibreglass so that their precise contours were recorded *in situ*. The stumps inside have probably rotted away by now, but the echoes of the trees live on like petrified elephant's legs striding through the trees at one end of West Dean gardens. Once Edward James was going to put statues on their tops, each holding a mirror to the other. But like so many of his schemes they blossomed only in his mind or on paper: somehow his life simply was not long enough to make all his fantasies reality.

Elephantine tree trunk memorials are unlikely ever to appear again at West Dean now that Edward James is dead. Ivan Hicks's small but astonishing eruption of oddity is one of the few areas of English garden where Edward James's spirit lives on. This eighteenth-century state of being, this proximity to the rich eccentric, brought out the eccentric in Ivan as well as a love for Magritte and Dali – hence the echoes of their pictures in his garden. But the pictures Ivan and Angie Hicks have created grow and move, and, much more, can be played in.

It is a puzzle why the Belgian surrealist painter Magritte should have had any effect at all on English gardens. There are two direct examples of his influence: Ivan Hicks's garden and the Surrealist Garden at Sutton Place, which is also sometimes known as the Magritte Garden. This is one small garden, no more than a walk in fact, set in the grounds of a Surrey manor. The grounds, which were landscaped by Sir Geoffrey Jellicoe, and the manor are presently being restored and so are not open to the public, but if they should reopen they are certainly worth a visit: the gardens are probably one of the largest, most spectacular and exciting pieces of twentieth-century English landscaping. There is a Paradise Garden, a huge walled garden with arbours and paths and windows looking out to the established and newly planted park land beyond; there is a moss garden, a wild garden and a garden created around a Ben Nicholson relief in white marble. There are plans for a series of cascades, too. The Magritte Garden is a walk enclosed by a formal hedge and a wall with vast stone urns of different sizes arranged down one side in such a way that they throw the vista out of perspective. In just the same way that the sky in Magritte's paintings and in Ivan Hicks's garden is painted with meticulous care and accuracy but juxtaposed or superimposed on unrelated objects, so the urns and the wall in the Sutton Place Magritte Garden are perfectly ordinary in their own right, but set out together as a scene they muddle the eye, if only for a moment. At the end of the walk there is a window flanked by two cypresses set in another brick wall showing trees beyond. The window looks strangely like a television screen, or a picture of a picture. As Magritte himself put it, 'If the spectator finds that my paintings are a kind of defiance of "common sense", he realizes something obvious. I want nevertheless to add that for me the world is a defiance of common sense.'

Charlie Boyle says he has never heard of Magritte, and yet there is an air of surrealism in his small garden outside his bungalow in the village of Thornleigh, just outside Leeds. What it lacks in size it makes up for in a riot of colour, decoration and the unexpected. There is a yellow rubber duck at the top of the Christmas tree. It is not Christmas and so, even if the rubber duck were of an angelic variety (which it is not), there is no reasonable excuse for such a decoration. The tree is a healthy specimen, thanks entirely (according to Charlie Boyle) to a regular pint of Tetley's beer. One of the few other living things in Charlie Boyle's garden is a mahonia which causes a certain amount of debate amongst passers by. When the leaves turn bright red some assume that this plant, like some of the rest of the garden, is made from plastic, porcelain, cement, rubber, or indeed anything so long as it contains not one living cell.

This debate gives Charlie Boyle great pleasure, as

does the continuing interest in his garden in this otherwise conventional village. A lavatory makes a startling centrepiece in the Boyle garden. In it floats a rubber duck who wears a headscarf when the weather gets cold. Even that is not nearly as startling as the green gloss-painted cistern which is decorated with a pair of Wellington boots and nailed to the front wall of the house overlooking the garden. For it is from this cistern that passers by, visitors and neighbours are serenaded with 'The Old Rugged Cross' and a selection of music-hall songs, some of them sung and recorded by Charlie himself, who was born in 1907. The music echoes mournfully out of the cistern across to the allotments opposite, where gardeners mulch Brussels sprouts and tend their dahlias. Even those who live in the bungalows on either side of Charlie Boyle's home steadfastly maintain pristine gardens in the face of the excesses of their neighbours.

Charlie Boyle is a bit lame. In fact his health is not good and this is something which distresses him greatly, if only because he feels he can't do justice to his garden. But how could Charlie's garden be better than it is? Many gardeners use colour, form or flower types as themes for their gardens. The duck is the theme in Charlie Boyle's garden, with almost anything made from plastic or rubber coming a close second. A display case on a plinth at the front of the garden shows a tableau of a big mother duck with six baby rubber ducks; on top of this a cart horse pulls a cart . . . containing a duck. To one side there is a blue-painted tank where another duck family floats idly. Sometimes another theme takes over from the duck because, like Ivan Hicks, Charlie Boyle likes to change and move his garden decoration from day to day. Even if it were not moved regularly the decoration and ornament would be eye-catching. A plastic donkey wearing protective industrial goggles heaves basket-loads of plastic flowers across the lawn. It would be futile to debate why there is a flipper hanging from the bird table or why blue-painted shoe lasts are used as ornaments. They are there for no other reason than they delight Charlie Boyle.

Some of the retaining walls for the flower beds are made from old razors, some from hundreds of used disposable razors; the ornaments include a clothes mangle (blue-glossed) which was such an excellent machine that Charlie still resents having turned it into an ornament; a miner's boot (blue-glossed); a meat-weighing machine (blue-glossed); a flat iron (blue-glossed); and a series of plastic ornamental tubs full of plastic flowers. One of the more macabre ornaments is a 'gateway to heaven' which lights up and was made by Charlie from a box, a doll and some special lighting. Hanging around Charlie's front door there is

THE RUBBER
DUCK AS A
HARD
LANDSCAPING
THEME

25

a festive collection of plastic flowers, a silver-painted shoe, and a pair of pink rubber gloves. The gloves have been stuffed, poked on to the ends of two six-foot poles and made to grasp bunches of plastic flowers as if they were dismembered bridesmaid's hands. Hanging on the outside wall just beside the front door is a Thermos flask with a light bulb poking out of the neck – although it doesn't work as a light. 'My doctor liked that. He was disappointed when I told him it didn't work,' says Charlie, putting 'The Old Rugged Cross' through the sound cistern again.

The doctor gets the blame for the garden. When Charlie Boyle's beloved wife died, Charlie, in his own words, 'took to bed for a week with a bottle'. His doctor recommended that he start an outside interest to take his mind off his troubles. Presumably the good doctor envisaged an appropriate hobby like bridge, stamp collecting, train spotting or growing prize marrows. Charlie Boyle decided he would indeed do something with his garden, although at this point the story becomes muddled because he insists, without explaining why, that he had to store a lavatory in his front garden. Having done so he felt it made an interesting effect – it certainly stimulated comment and interest from passers by, and this inspired him to rig up his cistern sound system. 'It gets a bit damp sometimes,' says Charlie Boyle, whose father was

sometimes the guard on the royal train on its way from London to Scotland for the King's northern holiday. 'The damp gets into the condensers so I have to keep the system inside in the winter. But it means I can change the music from inside and no one knows where it is coming from.'

'Some people say I'm a nutcase. But I just like decoration. People bring other people to see the garden.' He takes us inside his bungalow to read through some of the letters sent to him from all over the world by people who have visited and enjoyed the garden and its owner. Young and old appear to like the garden and return year after year to see it, and to see Charlie Boyle. Villagers seem used to being stopped in the street and asked the way to the 'lavatory garden'. 'Oh, you mean Charlie Boyle's. Up there, past the pub, left by the red van. He's quite a character you know,' they say with just a hint of trepidation.

His back garden is odd, too. It looks like the result of a scorched earth policy, except for one hellebore and a couple of hydrangeas which cower along one boundary. But nailed onto the fence opposite the bungalow there is a series of green-glossed car tyres in which plastic creepers have been planted. Their Hong Kong foliage spills out of the bottom inner edge of the tyre and down towards the soil: dreadful plastic wreaths on the grave of a living garden that never was.

ABOVE CHARLIE BOYLE WITH
HIS THERMOS AND LIGHT BULB

RIGHT ACROSS THE WAY FROM
THIS GARDEN MORE
MAINSTREAM STYLES OF
GARDENING PROVIDE
CONTRAST

Medusa's Gallery

When most people are asked about their garden gurus, the people who have inspired them to grow and cherish plants and to create great and small landscapes, the answers are predictable: parents, grandparents, Vita Sackville-West and her garden at Sissinghurst, Gertrude Jekyll, Robin Lane-Fox and his observations about gardens and gardening. Zandra Rhodes, dress designer to the extremely rich, gains her inspiration from Dickie Chopping, the man responsible for James Bond book covers. He has a splendid garden in Essex.

Zandra Rhodes's garden spreads vertically up four storeys of a terraced London house, starting from a tiny, sour soiled pit of a back yard. It began life soon after she bought her house in 1971, at a time when she knew nothing at all about gardens or gardening. Now when she wakes in her basement bedroom and peers through the wafts of pastel-coloured tulle around her bed, past the television suspended from the ceiling by golden chains and more tulle, she gazes through jasmine, a Swiss cheese plant and a philodendron on this side of the window to a tapestry of green and white planting on the other side. This is all her own work, her own design and her own execution. She used to have help with the maintenance, but she doesn't even have that now. It is clear that Zandra Rhodes, who is modest about her horticultural knowledge, has become an extraordinarily talented gardener, springing plants to life in this impossible pit of a garden.

To begin with the only living things in her shade-filled pit, apart from the streetwise cats who are the bane of her life, were a few miserable-looking ivies and a Russian vine. 'Ivies are not original for a shaded garden. But I didn't know that when I started. It wasn't that I didn't like gardening, I just didn't feel one way or the other about it,' she says. Now, though, the pit is awash with luxuriant planting: soft shield fern, *Polystichum setiferum* 'Densum', and the sensitive fern, *Onoclea sensibilis*, one foxglove (this must be a botanical record when you consider how readily foxgloves seed themselves), Solomon's seal, dogwood, pachysandra and one hundred lilies-of-the-valley. Then hellebores and hostas arrived, and with them a multitude of slugs. And they heralded the arrival of clever beer-filled green plastic slug traps, slug pubs. 'Gardeners' Question Time' told me I had to have a hedgehog to get rid of the slugs, so I got one called Humphrey. But he ran away after three days.'

The *Hydrangea petiolaris* and the climbing rose 'Golden Showers' sulked terribly when Zandra Rhodes first planted them, but then they scrambled up to the first floor of the house where they reached sunlight and air: now they flourish. There are azaleas and rhododendrons and a vine, possibly *Vitis coignetiae*, which blushes in the autumn, and a Russian vine, which is disciplined every three weeks to create swags at the back and at the front of the house along the top of some ironwork on the terrace. To complete the scene another set of plants makes a seasonal appearance, from April until the frosts, when they scurry inside for the winter: these tender specimens include spider plants, a miniature orange, stag's horn fern, *Platycerium bifurcatum*, and the tender and feathery fern, *Nephrolepis exaltata*, which can easily be mistaken for a plastic fern from a distance.

Zandra Rhodes has named this, the lower part of her plot, her green and white garden, which is misleading because the hard landscaping is brightly painted in the kinds of vivid colours used in her dress collections. Wild painting rampages over every hard surface, from the walls to some of the plant pots, which are covered with brightly coloured geometric patterns. A friend gave her a polystyrene Mexican Chac Mool, a reclining figure which, at eight feet long, was too big even for Zandra Rhodes's large house. So a steeply stepped altar or ziggurat was built in the yard and encrusted with jagged mirror pieces, and the Chac Mool was placed on top with the wall

behind painted vivid blue. And then Zandra Rhodes spotted some Hinduesque pillars at John Aspinall's gambling club and bought them, painted them in purples and pinks and yellows, and used them on either side of the altar and around the rest of the dank patch; and on top of these crazy ornaments she planted plastic ferns and plastic creepers. Along one wall she hung swags of scallop shells; the top of the highest walls, nearly twenty feet up, were decorated with empty terracotta pots. Once or twice a year, no more, on hot summer evenings, Zandra Rhodes covers the altar steps of her garden in cushions, and invites friends to have some supper with her and admire the garden. Otherwise the garden is seen and used only in snatches between work.

To reach the next stage of the garden, a first-floor terrace invisible from the basement garden, one has to go back through the basement living quarters. Here, like the rest of the house, there are constant and glorious reminders of Zandra Rhodes' obsession: pots of orchids, a ginger plant grown from a root sent to her by a friend in Hawaii, a vase of dogwood stems and lilies, and baskets of African violets mingling with a wood carving of a tree. A spiral staircase at the far end of the basement leads into a dining room of many colours and brightnesses. A huge chandelier drips with cut glass, a Dutch tulip pot displays lolling white

tulips on the table, and at the far end the polystyrene Chac Mool and his garden are framed in a porthole of window set in a wall of gold lamé. Past the multi-coloured entrance hall, up the stairs to the first landing where red oilskin curtains are swagged across a red sink. Through the floor-to-ceiling red-framed windows to a terrace where some more Mexican-style figures, this time Aztec-looking fibreglass dragon heads, sit in the middle of a series of pots which combine to make Zandra Rhodes' herb and fruit garden. There are red currants, lovage, chives, sage, mint (a great terracotta bowl brims with mint rhizomes, and in desperation Zandra Rhodes is threatening to throw it all away before it takes over her house and business) and sorrel: 'This is excellent for soup. I love cooking especially with things from my garden.'

On to the next bit of the garden, this time reached through French windows which open on to the narrow terrace at the front of the house. This is the Rose Terrace. Zandra Rhodes gets given a great number of plants, many of them roses. Each has to be assigned its proper place. There are miniature shrubs and climbing roses and a good old 'Mermaid', and yet more roses of every colour. And the rose garden gets used once a year as the spot at which Zandra Rhodes and her friends assemble for the Notting Hill carnival to

PILLARS FROM
A GAMBLING
CLUB –
SHOPPING FOR
GARDEN
DECORATION
CAN BE SO
MUCH MORE
FUN THAN A
TRIP TO THE
LOCAL
GARDEN
CENTRE

watch the floats rock by every August bank holiday.

Up more stairs and into a vast double-height room space with floor-to-roof windows at the very top of the house. A ladder is the only access. Here the sculptor Andrew Logan has his temporary studio. He is responsible for a Thing in the room behind the Rose Terrace: an abandoned ten-foot-high mirrored sculpture of a vaguely plantish shape. There are birds in cages, shapes and models of heavens knows what around the floors, and views of London. And it is here that Zandra Rhodes is planning to put her hanging gardens. Her circular bed will sit on a shelf beneath a circular window in the ceiling. The shelf will have one whole wall of window through to a conservatory alive with plants.

Every inch of available space in Zandra Rhodes's property has been utilized as garden. Even the window sills: the window boxes outside the dining room together make up the Yellow Garden, with pale yellow hyacinths and yellow daffodils, even if they do clash a little with the pink camellias which have been planted in the well below and the pink-painted façade of the house.

Zandra Rhodes has mingled sculpture, colour and form to brighten her otherwise dark and impossible plot. She has blended plants and sculpture together to create a unified vision quite unlike the effect in some sculpture parks, where the hard and soft landscaping can appear to be totally unrelated. In Zandra Rhodes's garden the sculpture and the plants do not seem at odds with one another. She encourages the effect by letting the bright paintwork fade and crumble just a little as if it is about to be devoured, destroyed and overtaken by the vigorous growth all about it.

She does all this by squeezing her garden activities into long working days. Take a typical Sunday morning for instance: she has been up since five thirty pruning her magnolia and buddleia, her bright pink hair glinting in the sunlight. Zandra says she usually only gets about four hours of sleep in every twenty-four, although whenever she sits down and relaxes she tends to cat nap. If it were not for her business she would spend all day every day pottering around her garden.

Now when she whirls around the world – Japan, Italy, the States, South America, from fashion show to art gallery to glitterati party – she sidles off when she can to shady areas to find new plants which will thrive in her garden. 'I was up in the Himalayas and saw this *Magnolia stellata*. It was huge and beautiful and I thought that if it could grow up there where it was cold it would be all right in London.' And that is her key: she finds out where a plant comes from and the conditions in which it thrives naturally and she then decides whether or not she can match those conditions.

One of Zandra's gardening friends gave her a double white camellia which was planted in a huge terracotta urn and put in the back garden. That turned her on to camellias and now there are four: a pale, almost white pink, a red and two more pink-flowering bushes in the sub-basement at the front of the house. The gardening bug has taken root, grown and flourished in Zandra Rhodes, and yet the odd thing is that there isn't one specimen of her favourite plant, the stinging nettle. She made a detailed drawing of one while she was at college and fell in love with the plant. She is also in love with the plant immortalized on the tops of Corinthian columns, the acanthus, and hopes to grow it. Most of all she is excited by the challenge of having to make a splendid, all-year-round garden against all the odds: no acid soil for the camellias, so they live in containers; no sun; no space, so the garden has to continue up the walls.

Her devotion to gardening is complete. She has 'Gardeners' Question Time' tapes and listens to the programme religiously; she has several shelves full of gardening books, and in just the way that most people have garden sheds Zandra Rhodes has a garden cupboard on her first floor, where the broom, dustpans, dusters and all the house cleaning materials are shelved neatly alongside every conceivable kind of fertilizer, weed killer, insecticide, spray and garden tool. There is a serious compost heap to one side of the polystyrene Chac Mool, into which all household and garden refuse is put to rot, but that is the extent of her organic gardening.

The following garden belongs to Jan Wright, the sculptor, another woman whose professional life is devoted to form and shape and colour. The sculpture in her front garden is thought by some to create such an incongruous effect that it should not be allowed; they feel that there is such an uneasy relationship between the garden and the sculpture that it is not quite proper. More to the point, some say, is that the sculpture is, well, rude.

The view from Jan Wright's symmetrical thirties house in the genteel seaside town of Worthing is of a bottom. An enormous concrete bottom which will be familiar to anyone who went to the Glasgow Garden Festival. 'Reclining Woman' by Dhruva Mistry, sponsored by British Shipbuilders, is missing the uppermost section of her head and her legs below the knee (she was made that way) but she still measures 7 feet 10 inches by 7 feet 4 inches by thirteen feet (2.3 × 2.2 × 3.9 metres) and weighs five tons, which is an awkward kind of size and weight to handle: hardly the average garden gnome weight or birdbath size for instance. This meant that when it came to auctioning off all the statuary from the Glasgow Garden Festival, the lovely Reclining Woman, with rust red eyes and darkened lips and red edged nipples standing cherry-like on top of perfect dome-like bosoms, was rejected. It is hard to believe because she is a marvellous, voluptuous sight: so coy, so naughty and so appealing, her resting hip almost as high as the front door. No one would have her, until a landscape consultant, Wilf Simms, read an article in *The Independent* describing the Glasgow Garden Festival statuary which had failed to reach its reserve at a Christie's auction. At just the time when she was being rejected, he was being accepted as a future husband by Jan Wright. Both had seen the statue and liked it, and so it was that Wilf bought Jan the Reclining Woman as an engagement gift, for the knock-down price of £16,000 plus £2,000 VAT. Allowing £2,000 for the handling and transport of this hard beauty, Reclining Woman was a snip at a total of £20,000. She was also very much a gift for Jan's garden, which was in keeping with all Wilf's presents to Jan, beginning with a *Prunus subhirtella* 'Autumnalis'.

But whatever could be said to be the artistic merits of Wilf's engagement present, her arrival in Worthing brought fury and controversy to Jan and Wilf's pre-nuptial life. They could never have predicted the fuss that was to come when a crane lowered Reclining Woman into their front garden. She had at first been valued at £30,000 and, as one of Jan's neighbours pointed out once or twice, even for the knock-down price she eventually fetched Wilf could have bought Jan a really nice car instead. But as Jan says, everyone has a car but who has a five-ton sculpture in her quarter-acre front garden?

Other front gardens in this respectable area are of the hydrangea and hebe variety, or of the camper van or caravan variety, either of which is regarded as perfectly proper. Wilf calls them 'dinky doo' gardens: gardens as neat as a fitted carpet. Jan's garden is now no longer regarded as respectable, even though passers by on the pavement outside have to stand on tiptoe and peek through the skimmia to see Reclining Woman on her bed of steel girders. It is not as if she is intrusive on the street. The soft landscaping of plants, on the other hand, is probably one of the most respectable in the street. Jan has retained a lot of the original garden: the box on either side of the door, the holly, the ceanothus and bay, the double white lilac, the rockery, the beech and the apple trees twined together like lovers, the laurels, the myrtles. She has

WILF SIMMS, JAN WRIGHT AND PART OF THE
RECLINING WOMAN SCULPTURE WHICH LANGUISHES
ACROSS THEIR FRONT GARDEN IN WORTHING

THE VIEW FROM
JAN WRIGHT'S
FRONT DOOR

added – only if and when plants have to be replaced – specialist plants given to her by Wilf, such as the rare *Buddleia lindleyana* and the white willow, *Salix alba* 'Maculata' (syn. *Salix integras* 'Hakuro-nishiki').

Wilf's knowledge of plants is breathtaking. He has won prizes as well as fame for his specialist expertise. Today he is above all an arid zone specialist. He has created gardens and football pitches in Saudi Arabia, has helped with large landscaping schemes at the palace gardens of the Sultan of Oman, and has advised the Nigerian and Zambian governments on planting. He has travelled the world at the request of both governments and individuals, helping people with tricky planting problems, and now he is the managing

WILF SIMMS'S
ANSWER TO GARDEN
GNOMES

director of a large landscaping firm based in London. And although Wilf specializes in arid zone plants he is interested in a wide variety of plants, a fact reflected in his wife's garden. All kinds of jasmine flourish in it. There are at least sixty varieties of potentilla, one of the plants in which Wilf specializes, his favourite being *Potentilla rhodocalyx*, as well as several varieties of pittosporum and *Weigela* 'Ruby Gold', which has gold foliage and deep pink flowers. In the conservatory which has just been built at the back of the house there is an unusual collection of scented-leaved pelargoniums and some shrubs from the Middle East.

Jan and Wilf have created a Japanese garden at the back of the Reclining Woman. Not that there is much choice; between her bottom and the front of the house there isn't much sunlight, so pebbles and stone lanterns and a few azaleas and bamboos are just the thing. This area of the garden grows black-stemmed bamboos which arrived when they were twelve feet tall, tied with red ribbon and a 'Happy Birthday' label from Wilf to Jan. The rest of the garden in which Reclining Woman languishes has a slightly suburban woodland feel to it. It is planted with dwarf rhododendrons, camellias, magnolia and that lovely pale green evergreen shrub *Griselinia*, which will grow only in mild, sheltered coastal gardens. A glossy leaved relation of hawthorn, the white-flowered *Crataegus* × *lavallei*, stands along one of the boundaries, and there are also bay, Cistus, the grey-leaved aromatic shrub *Teucrium fruticans* and hydrangeas.

The problem is that although you have to be pretty nosy to see Reclining Woman from the street, she has stirred up such extreme feelings that she cannot be ignored, however well camouflaged. Not since the 'Rite of Spring', perhaps, has one work of art caused such spontaneous mass objection and comment. Some people feel the sculpture isn't quite the right form of decoration for the area, some say it is obscene, ghastly and grotesque, others say that it simply doesn't fit there in a suburban garden. One resident is rumoured to have threatened to refuse to pay local rates on the strength of the offence allegedly caused by Reclining Woman. Some people are now trying to see if they can get rid of the Reclining Woman by insisting on planning permission for her.

There are others who have hurt the Reclining Woman's body as opposed to her reputation: hooligans who jumped up and down on the vast sculpture managed to crack her stomach, although not seriously. So now Jan and Wilf have built sturdy fences with locked gates around their property, and they may install security spotlights. They may also simply go back to their original plan for Reclining Woman and take her up to Orkney, where Wilf has a home, where there is more space and, with a bit of luck, greater tolerance. Will the islanders feel that Reclining Woman is erotic, and if they do will they be offended by that? This seems to be one of the main objections from some residents of Worthing. Certainly her pert bosoms have echoes of Indian erotic art, but only the tiniest hint – hardly a sculptured version of one of the *Kama Sutra*'s steamy scenes.

In one sense Reclining Woman fits perfectly with Jan's garden. She bought the property in 1986, before she met Wilf, and in the summer holidays when she wasn't teaching art at a nearby college she used to move some of her sculptures out into the front garden, there to mingle with the hornbeam hedges,

A LARGE
CONCRETE
BOTTOM
CASTS SHADOW
OVER THIS
PART OF THE
GARDEN

OWLBERT THE ORNAMENTAL
OWL IN JAN AND WILF'S
GARDEN

sculptures were considerably smaller than Reclining Woman so nobody was made to feel that she was letting the side down. Perhaps they would have felt differently if they could have seen some of the rest of the landscaping details in the garden: dangling prism mirrors and a wooden parrot in the trees, an ornamental owl called Owlbert who lives in a tree, and dozens of frogs and a few newts, the latter real with permanent residence in the pond. There are concrete animals, too: squirrels, rabbits and cats, which inhabit the garden, but all hidden by a rich mix of plants, some unusual, such as *Kerria* 'Guinea Gold', *Spiraea* 'Bella', *S.* 'Snowhite'; phlomis and a *Ginkgo biloba*.

If Jan and Wilf had established their garden in Cornwall they might have been left alone. Cornwall is much more than a county, it is an unproclaimed independent state where eccentricity in the material and spiritual world are almost always accepted with equanimity. Which may be why Ed Prynn's garden has been allowed to flourish without hindrance. It is difficult to know where to begin with Ed Prynn. He is a Cornishman born and bred, so it is no good trying to picture him as an Englishman. Like the Welsh and the Scottish, the Cornish are a breed apart, and very proud of it. When I lived there I came across quite a few people who had never crossed the

periwinkle, aquilegia, yucca, her iris collection (some of the plants grown from seed) and a twisted ash. So she was already laying the foundations for a sculpture garden. But the point was that few could really see these sculptures from the road because they were planted under a useful canopy of fruit trees. And Jan's

Tamar, the river that divides Cornwall from Devon ('the mainland'), and one old lady who had never been more than a mile or so outside her village. Why should she bother? There is an independent streak which runs through many Cornish people, born partly from their geographical position on a great peninsula jutting out into the sea, partly from a sense of solidarity in the face of the threat of the surprisingly treacherous seas on the north and south coasts and at Land's End, and partly in response to the necessary nuisance caused by tourists and weekenders.

Once Ed Prynn was a shovel driver in a quarry. Now, after many adventures, including writing books and heaven knows what, he has made a Mystical Garden or open-air Druids' Temple outside his modern bungalow on the north coast of Cornwall. It is a small garden flanked by a wall of conifers on one side. There is no room for flowers here, and instead the lawn erupts with standing stones like Stonehenge or Avebury Circle or some of the West Country stones on Bodmin Moor and Dartmoor. Ed Prynn's more recent addition to the standing stone tradition is made by a ring of seven stones carved out of one gigantic chunk of granite from nearby St Breward. Each monolith from that original stone now represents one of the women in Ed's life, including his mother Marjorie, Monica, the Secret Lady, and his

great aunt Hilda. There is a Holy Well, pierced into the earth where, so Ed says, a diviner found water crossing a ley line; there is an Angels' Runway, the largest stone in the collection; a Judgement Stone; a Healing Stone and a Marriage Stone over which Ed Prynn has conducted marriage ceremonies. Not real marriage ceremonies: the couple is usually married already but in need of a cementing ceremony on their anniversary. All the same, the 'brides' tend to wear white, and in order to make the ceremonies seem more authentic, Ed Prynn has bought some Jesse Jackson tapes to learn how to preach. He believes in doing things properly. The bride and groom stand either side of the marriage stone, which has a hole through it, and then at the end of the ceremony they are allowed to hold hands and then to kiss. It is an excellent place for the renewal of such pledges: a place of tranquillity perched on a hill outside the village proper, reached by a narrow lane which heaves with the scent of honeysuckle throughout June and July.

This yen to build monuments and move magnificent stones into prominent positions started when Ed Prynn was nine years old, exploring the Cornish moors. He came across one of the rings of standing stones and heard the story behind it: some people went to dance on the moor on a Sunday, the day of rest, and were turned to stone as punishment. The fascination

Eccentric Gardens

STANDING STONES WITH ED PRYNN'S
BUNGALOW IN THE BACKGROUND

Medusa's Gallery

ED PRYNN'S
ROCK GARDEN

that began then grew and festered until it cried out to be made into reality. The materialization of this dream has not been without its practical problems. Ganger men, and forty-five-ton cranes and JCBs have been used to move some of the stones into position in the back garden. When the first rock arrived, weighing ten tons or so, Ed Prynn felt that with the help of a low loader he would be able to handle it on his own. He was wrong, but only just: he manoeuvred it into place with the help of two pensioners.

Ed Prynn still lives with his mother and father on the council estate where they have lived for very many years. He likes it there, he knows all the people and they all know him, and although his brand new whitewashed bungalow and his marvellous garden are waiting for him to inhabit them, he can't bring himself to move in. His greatest ambition now is to build a monument bigger than Stonehenge on one of the nearby moors, a monument which will represent the ten commandments. 'Even if people aren't religious, the ten commandments are good rules to live by,' he says. He is in the process of building a tunnel of fame for all the people who have helped him with his standing stone project. He will mine a tunnel underneath his front garden and line it with huge slates, each carved with the name of one of the people who have helped. The more they have helped, the more likely it

THE MARRIAGE STONE, WHERE COUPLES RENEW THEIR VOWS

will be that pictures of archangels (as opposed to mere angels) will be carved next to their name.

Mrs Thatcher's name will be carved in the tunnel of fame because Ed Prynn says she visited his garden on one of the Cornish golfing holidays she and her husband enjoy. Rex Hunt, the governor of the Falklands Islands at the time of the Argentinian invasion, will also be remembered in the tunnel, because he is responsible for having shipped one vast stone from Mount Pleasant on the Falkland Islands to Ed Prynn. Ed Prynn explained why but, like so many of his stories, it seemed to involve so many coincidences and so many quite outrageous requests on his behalf which were miraculously granted, that in a sense the story is best left simple: Ed Prynn felt that a stone from the Falklands was a crucial element missing from his garden, and so stone from the Falklands materialized. It could only happen to a Cornishman like Ed Prynn.

ED PRYNN
UNDER THE
ANGELS'
RUNWAY IN HIS
CORNISH
GARDEN

Liquidity:
The Affording of Water Gardens

Lord Snowdon, the owner of two unusual gardens, one in Sussex and one in London, is something of a hard landscaping magician, although he proudly announces that he is not a gardener. Christopher Masson, former assistant to the late Lanning Roper, looks after the planting in this city garden. Snowdon himself knows no flower names, none, and he will not countenance coloured flowers in his London garden. Despite that, some fuchsia and nasturtium flowers are bravely waving dazzling colours from an otherwise all-green and white garden. His garden is an exercise in making a shady, sheltered back yard into an elegant and soothing retreat from the world. Snowdon's garden passion manifests itself in some peculiar bits of hard landscaping rather than in any planting flights of fancy. He likes designing, inventing and constructing artefacts to make his garden entertain as well as please.

'I am not a gardener AT ALL,' he says, and then pays tribute to his gardening family, which includes Ludwig Messel and his descendants, creators of Nymans in Sussex, one of England's finest gardens. 'But I like architectural follies,' says Snowdon and points to something which his family regard as his greatest folly. At the centre of his small L-shaped garden in Kensington there is a pond, and at the centre of that there stands a large classical urn. All of which is pretty ordinary, but poised above the urn, mid-air, hawk-like and apparently unsupported, there is a wine bottle that splashes clear water into the stone bowl. It is a curious sight, but perhaps for someone like Snowdon, who is used to stately homes where the gardens take themselves terribly seriously, this was a welcome relief. Unfortunately the wine bottle water trick is unpopular and so it spends most of its time out of sight.

'Everyone loathed the bottle. I just shoved a tube of clear perspex from the water source in the bowl of the urn into the bottle to create the effect. Water was pumped up through the tube and splashed down again in such a way that it concealed the perspex tube and made it look as if the bottle were supported by water. Everything needs to be sent up, that's what it's all about. The urn was much too serious. People take gardens too seriously. But everyone, all my family, really hated the bottle so it came down,' says Snowdon, who has since exhibited this ingenious device at the Brighton Pavilion.

The garden, which is reached by walking through

EVEN THE BUST CAN'T BELIEVE HIS EYES.
SUSPENSION OF DISBELIEF AND A BOTTLE IN
LORD SNOWDON'S LONDON GARDEN

AN OWL AS A
BIRD SCARER
PROVED HOPELESS

the house, past the studio and darkroom and the red-painted, wood-panelled office, is lush and enclosed by huge limes hugging the boundaries to create peace and privacy. An old hawthorn outside Snowdon's studio provides a perch for an elegant grey plastic owl. 'That is my answer to garden gnomes. Every garden should have garden gnomes. That is mine. Actually it was meant to scare pigeons but it attracts them like mad. The plastic ducks are important too.' He is referring to some decoy ducks, floating sedately in the pond around which Christopher Masson has added a neat box hedge edge and a gravel path. Snowdon is a great designer and maker of things, always wanting to change, to invent and experiment. He waves towards a corner of the garden which is filled with laurel, lime and birch, saying he thinks it looks rather boring and that it needs something in it, so he may design a little folly.

No doubt he will design one and then make it himself, like the rows of balustrades which edge a small height change in the garden. Like the veranda he has made by the door which leads from his studio in the garden. The ornate Victorian iron lace and ornamentation along the edge of the veranda fits beautifully with the decoration on the rest of the house.

Close by the house stands Snowdon's favourite piece of garden furniture, which comes from his uncle Oliver Messel. The heavy marble table top is carried on a great twist, a knot, of ironwork. Some of the rest of the garden furniture came from an old Bradford bandstand, and the sturdy Edwardian iron and wood seats have been painted a deep, dusty olive green, which is a colour Snowdon likes but hopes to develop into the perfect green: unobtrusive, elegant and fitting for a garden. 'I'm very anti-white when it comes to garden furniture. I hate all that white stuff,' he says.

Snowdon gives the impression that, even as he speaks, his mind is whizzing through the viability of yet another crazy or not-so-crazy garden scheme. A few years ago he wanted an extra summer house away

THE PAVILION,
ONE OF
SNOWDON'S
DESIGNS

HARD AND SOFT LANDSCAPING
IN SNOWDON'S GARDEN. THE
DUCKS ARE PART OF THE
FORMER

from the main house, so he made himself a funny turret like a free-standing room at one corner of the garden. A massive lime tree grows up the centre of the room, through the roof and out into the open air. Snowdon couldn't bear to fell the lime so he designed a circular room which was built around the tree. Then he added a second room beside the first, with a Gothic door and an elegantly domed copper roof with flame like leaves of copper flying up from the top. He constructed a detailed scale model of the turret room in card before beginning the real building work, and then he ingeniously devised the building in such a way that rain water is channelled down the lime tree to water the roots.

Outside again he explains how he made a spouting wall decoration by covering a grotesque mask he found in the Kings Road, Chelsea in a special Bath stone dust and concrete mix. Then he drilled holes in the eyes so the mask cries fountain tears into the semicircular pool below. Snowdon's garden is predominantly, beautifully green. 'I like everything to be green and white. It is a green oasis. I like it to stay the same from one season to the next. In a way this garden is very influenced by my uncle Oliver Messel's garden in Barbados. I like it looking like a jungle. A man came to see me the other day, and when he saw the garden he said, "Oh you're like me. You've done

the house but you haven't got round to the garden yet."' He stifles his chuckles in a tirade about the importance of good lighting in a garden. 'Lighting is terribly important, don't you think? It's best to back-light everything. You just shove lights into old Ovaltine tins with the bottoms cut out, and that directs light so you don't see the source.'

Snowdon's main garden preoccupation at the moment is the digging up of an intricate knot garden which he created in his Sussex garden in the sixties. It is going to be replaced with a series of cascades. 'Nothing stays the same in gardens, I like doing something new and funny all the time. When I couldn't get planning permission to build a larger studio across here into the garden I decided instead to make the outside look like a Tasmanian railway station.' So now there is an outside wall where vaguely Antipodean railway embellishments have been added. I wonder what Lanning Roper would have made of the Railway Station look.

'Lanning Roper, who is one of this country's really great gardeners and a man for whom I have the greatest admiration, was involved in designing and planting some of this garden. Most of the planting has stayed as he planned it,' says Lord Snowdon. 'I suppose it's a bit like getting Capability Brown to do your window box.'

THE WEEPING
MASK

THE ENGLISH COUNTRY GARDEN

Year-round colour and interest in a garden is an ideal to which many gardeners aspire but which few achieve. Clifford Davis has become part of the minority – albeit by an unconventional method, because every inch of his plot is made from plastic, concrete or wood. This synthetic garden took root a good few years ago, when so-called spring was even longer in coming than usual. Clifford's fine planting of real daffodils showed only as a sea of deep green spikes, which made him maudlin and impatient for a little colour and action in his garden. As he paced his home town, St Anne's, a seaside stroll away from Blackpool, he spotted a plastic daffodil abandoned in a neighbouring dustbin. Taking mercy on this once proud flower he picked it from the bin, brought it home and painted it to bring out its bright, floral qualities.

Then he stuck it in the midst of the little green shoots which were being so tardy about showing any flower. The painted daff shone beacon-like, almost brassy in Holfield Road, St Anne's. After the one daff beginning, the garden grew almost organically, spreading from a window box of flowers to a bed below the sill. Then the boring old bed at the front of the house was replaced with a luminescent green corrugated plastic 'lawn' from which more flowers and tufts of plastic grass could grow. The privet hedge fell from favour too, and in its place Clifford made a green-painted wooden wall with shelves for rows of flowers. There is a great deal to see in this curious garden. Apart from the manic colours of the flowers, the spindly sunflower type plants to one side of the door and the relentlessly plastic garden, the structure of each flower is a marvel. He makes the centre of each flower with slashed and splayed-out sauce bottle tops, wire and plastic cotton reels. Then, by melting coloured plastic discs into floral submission by dipping them in hot water he creates orchids, marguerites, sunflowers, mysterious creeping flowers and roses. The final touch is created by two ponds in the centre of the lawn. Not any old ponds but duck ponds ... with plastic ducks. The ducks bob pleasingly in a gentle breeze.

'You should see people's faces when they see the garden. Youngsters like it. They come and have a look. You can't get them away from the end of the garden.' Passers by certainly stop and stare. Some, the short-sighted perhaps, believe this to be a strangely vivid display of real flowers.

Clifford watches the reactions from his front room window. He is delighted to be causing such a stir. He is seventy-seven years old, and has lived an odd sort of life: miner as a lad, a north London café owner; a fish and chip bar owner; the failed inventor in 1967 of the flying bicycle; a farmer near Wakefield and a milkman. Making a stir again is quite a pleasure even if it has meant getting rid of his old, natural garden. Anyway, real flowers are so – unpredictable, flighty even. Not like plastic flowers on which you can rely. And by making his own plastic flowers, not only could Clifford fill his garden with colour, he could also watch over his bedridden wife as he worked. He bought coloured plastic bowls, fabric conditioner bottles, petrol cans and plastic objects of all descriptions. Friends brought him all the coloured plastic they could lay their hands on. 'I go scrounging in the dustbins before the dustbin men come round,' he says, as we sit in his front room peeping between plastic ferns set this side of the window and plastic flowers set the other side of the window to the world beyond, where the garden has flourished from one plastic daff to a great sea of brightly coloured synthetic flowers.

The neighbours aren't sure about Clifford's garden. For this sort of thing to happen in Blackpool is one thing, but St Anne's, some feel, is too respectable for such an outrageous display. A couple in a red Ford Escort drive by and then reverse up again, incredulous at what they have seen. Is Clifford Davis sniggering or simply readjusting his floral cravat? I shall never know

CLIFFORD DAVIS FOUND MOTHER NATURE TO BE
AN UNRELIABLE SOURCE OF COLOUR AND FORM 58

because he is now in full flood explaining that in order to find fortune in this world there is only one path to take: sell plastic duck ponds, like his own, the secret of which is a shower tray. 'That's all that pond is. A plastic shower tray. You don't have to paint it. You can put them in just like that. People all over the country will be wanting them.' Floating beside the ducks there is a dazzling yellow Jiff lemon painted bright red at one end. I quizz Clifford about this addition. 'Yes, it's a plastic lemon with some paint on,' he says. So there we are.

Glancing along the rows of orange-painted cotton reels (in other words, the central trumpets of the daffs growing in mid-air up the green-painted boundary wall) the eye is attracted down to a second, smaller pond. In it there are some more rubber ducks. And a doll's head floating eerily on the surface. Questions about The Head bring the Jiff lemon response. 'They used to call me Henry Moore,' says Clifford Davis. Who? Why? 'The local papers. I used to be a sculptor. But I threw away all my sculptures.'

We are back in his front room with a dog at our knees. The dog is concrete and painted bright yellow. The story of the plastic takeover changes slightly: 'During the miners' strike we got so fed up with seeing news about the miners and how many men had been laid off, we decided to sell the telly. I took it back

to the shop on the corner. It was the best thing we ever did. But in the space it left we wanted something to look at so we went into town to get lots of flowers. Fabric flowers. They look lovely. Much nicer than the telly.'

They are still there, along with the plastic flowers in the inside glass door in the hall, and the plastic and fabric flowers decorating the walls throughout the downstairs of the house. We go to the greenhouse. Very properly, this is where Clifford makes his flowers. It is a lean-to greenhouse at the back of the house without a trace of any living thing. Just buckets of bowls and Squeezy bottles with bits cut out of them. Clifford's flowers would have found a place in Edward Lear's Nonsense Botany as *Plasticus plasticus*. Or perhaps the nonsense poet had already allowed for them with his curious hybrid *Washtubbia circulasis*. This imaginary flower comes complete with an illustration of a flower which looks remarkably like a wash tub gently nodding on the end of stalk and leaves.

The Victorians, deprived of the possibility of using plastic to make flowers, had to make do with risqué planting jokes like growing maidenhair next to bachelor's buttons. But one late Victorian, E. A. Bowles, who was a serious botanist

SOMETIMES A PLASTIC LEMON AND A DOLL'S HEAD
JOIN THE DUCKS IN THE POOL. SOMETIMES THE
DOLL'S HEAD GAZES INTO THE POOL INSTEAD

and alpine expert, cleared an area in the garden of the house where he was born, Myddleton Hall in north London, and called it his 'Lunatic Asylum'. Here, where stuck-up laurel once grew, Bowles (or Gussie as he was known to his chums) planted any demented plants that came his way. An extremely twisted hazel given to him by a Canon Ellacombe was followed by a twisted hawthorn, and that was followed by an elder with a particularly feathery look. Then came a laburnum which was trying hard to look like an oak, hence *Laburnum quercifolium*, and 'vulgar' because the leaves had decided to crinkle up.

Bertha Richardson has no need for plastic flowers or for horticultural peculiarities in her tiny garden because it is crammed full of thousands of the real thing: perfect, home-grown bedding plants. She has made floral excess into an art form. Once Bertha Richardson had roses in her garden. But the shape and size of her plot – seventy-five feet long and twelve feet wide – meant that she had to take them out because the hordes of annual visitors to her narrow garden were getting caught up in the thorns. Hers is not a likely place for a prize-winning garden, just down the road from Barnsley in Yorkshire and squeezed between the pit head and a row of miners' cottages. This is one of the most abundant gardens you are ever likely to see. It has proved that where there isn't the flat acreage to make displays, gardening up fences, hedges and walls is just as effective.

A path runs from the back door to some small sheds at the back of the garden, and just outside the back door stands the garden's most expensive addition so far – a conservatory which was first prize in a magazine competition (gardening, of course). The trellis down part of the boundary wall beside the house is made from old broken-up cauliflower boxes. Along one side of the garden splendid great arches, heavy with flowers, screen neighbouring gardens: the arches are made from strips of bamboo originally used as part of the packaging for Japanese motor cycles. And the hoops which complete the top of the left-hand boundary are made from hoola hoops, still a sore point with Bertha who had to pay full price for them. Along the walls there are hundreds of grey plastic pot-holders which support hundreds of yoghurt pots of bedding plants like busy lizzies (impatiens), salvias or geraniums. The pot-holders are made from slices of grey plastic drain pipe nailed to the wall. The planting is echoed in side beds and island beds engulfed with bedding plants.

Bertha's garden is a reminder of how it is possible to create a superb display on almost nothing. She is

BERTHA AND NORMAN RICHARDSON
IN THEIR GARDEN

seventy-four years old and retired, although her idea of retirement means getting up at six o'clock every day to work on her garden; it means learning about calligraphy; it means being a mainstay of the church and the local amateur dramatic society as well as painting in oils. Thus, every plant comes from seed from previous years or from cuttings, and all one thousand or more bedding plants are grown with the help of an eight foot by four foot unheated makeshift lean-to greenhouse at the back of the garage, and yoghurt pots of seedlings and plants on every window sill throughout the two-up–two-down cottage.

Until 1964 the garden was a cross between Hades and an adventure playground for local children. It was the year that Bertha and Norman decided to buy the house where Bertha had been born. No sooner had they set up home together than Bertha started work on the garden. The soil was sour and impregnated with coal dust and so they began by buying in one ton of topsoil, and since then they have added a ton of manure every year. Living near so many farms has its advantages.

'I was fed up with looking at the pit head. I wanted lots of colour. It's like a shout of defiance. I get the garden to shout "Look at me",' says Bertha, who does not seem like a defiant sort of person at all, just a regular potty gardener. But then if her garden is being defiant on her behalf perhaps she behaves in a more seemly fashion. Neither Bertha nor Norman knew anything about gardens and so through trial and error they grew everything they could from cuttings given to them by gardener friends. They collected hedge trimmings from an allotment nearby and from the cuttings grew a privet hedge down the whole of the right-hand side of the garden. This they sculpted into elegant scallop shapes by hanging the washing line against it and cutting great curves out of the top of the hedge along precisely the course where the washing line curved.

ABOVE THE CONSERVATORY
WAS A PRIZE – THIS GARDEN IS
MADE ON A TIGHT BUDGET

RIGHT BERTHA RICHARDSON'S
RIOTOUS DISPLAY OF BEDDING
IS ESPECIALLY REMARKABLE IN
GOLDTHORPE, WHERE PIT
HEAD VIEWS (IN THE
DISTANCE) ARE THE NORM

Eccentric Gardens

The garden prospered and grew in abundance until it started to win prizes. The Mayor of Barnsley visited it and gave them a silver cup and a speech. Local newspapers started writing features about Bertha's garden and so she started to open to raise money for her favourite charities. There was only one problem. Bertha painted white lines along the edges of the path running down the garden to keep her visitors on the straight and narrow, but it soon became clear that the garden was so narrow only a few people at a time could be let in. The rest had to hover in the kitchen before they could sidle down the path. The house still becomes a quasi waiting room for the garden whenever Norman and Bertha open it to the public. Apart from the roses which were excluded because they caused problems to visitors, certain other plants like nicotiana had to be ruled out because they grew high and bushy enough to tangle with people and their handbags. And, after all, what's the point in growing senseless scentless dwarf varieties?

Most other gardens in the area are dingy by comparison. There is nothing quite like Bertha's garden near any other pit head. It is a surprise, even a shock for the uninitiated, to come across such abundance in the middle of a depressed mining town. So how does she manage to create such a paradise in the middle of such gloom? Is it chatting to the plants? No, she

IT TAKES SEVERAL THOUSAND PLANTS, GROWN FROM SEED OR CUTTINGS EACH YEAR, TO MAKE THIS DISPLAY. VISITORS HAVE DIFFICULTY SQUEEZING IN

doesn't go along with that, although once when a honeysuckle that Bertha had bought from Lord Halifax's place refused, year after year, to flower, Norman stood in front of it and announced: 'Right, we'll cut it down.' Two weeks later it flowered. That was an exception to the rule, and generally good honest graft and muck keeps Bertha Richardson's garden lovely.

The Victorian idea of plant loveliness, bedding out, which has been so cleverly adapted by Bertha Richardson for the late twentieth century, is used in more traditional form by Stan Clark in the west country. He uses bedding to celebrate major royal events such as weddings or the birth of a baby. Local people and the local press know that if Buckingham Palace announce a birth, Stan Clark's garden will be well worth a visit. When England's future king, Prince William, arrived, Stan's garden was awash with baby pastel shades of pink and blue alyssum, lobelia and petunias. Just above the names CHARLES, DIANA, WILLIAM, which were etched into the lawn, was a magnificent stork-shaped bed of white alyssum. In its beak the stork, quite properly, carried a basket (again of alyssum) with a baby doll in it.

In 1988 the garden was re-landscaped to honour the birth of Princess Beatrice, the daughter of the Duke and Duchess of York. This time the stalk was three-dimensional and made from silver foil wrapped around lengths of wood. Originally Stan Clark had wanted to etch the names out in lines of alyssum but the lines grew too abundant, melted together and couldn't be read. So the names ANDREW, SARAH,

BEATRICE were raised in silver foil letters, while above them a round bed displayed a floral Union Jack in lobelia, alyssum and salvia. Gnomes around the pond witnessed this event, and the air of celebration was extended by Union Jacks fluttering from the hedges.

'Crowds gather at the end of my garden when I plant it out specially,' says Stan Clark, who is a textile worker specializing in making the cloth for tennis balls. 'It started because I was in the Navy and I became royalty mad. I'd do anything for royalty. When the Queen had her jubilee year I decided to lay the garden out specially for her. I'm just an amateur gardener, I don't know the names of any of the plants and I have to buy them instead of growing them from seed. The plants cost me about £60 but it's worth it for royalty.' To complete the royal effect of this small garden, just down the road from the homes of the Princess Royal and the Prince and Princess of Wales, Stan has castellated the surrounding hedges.

Royalty seem to approve of this unusual way of celebrating their family events. Although Stan has never met any of them, and although none has visited his garden, he has sent pictures of his garden to the palace. And ladies-in-waiting and equerries have sent letters full of thanks and praise on behalf of their royal masters and mistresses. Stan Clark has the thick, red-crested letters to prove it.

Noble Landscapes and One Folly

To reach Faringdon House you make your way through the small Oxfordshire market town of Faringdon, between two sturdy Cotswold stone pillars, along a curve of gravel bordered by a spring garden of hyacinths, tulips, *Anemone blanda* and narcissi (a planting which is now copied around many gardens in the south of England) to the elegant eighteenth-century house. This is all so very correct, polite and predictable that if an aged colonel or a gum-booted landowner were to appear, all would be well and everything would be pigeonholed neatly into the Rich County Squire slot. However, instead of a greeting from a ruddy-faced member of the gentry the visitor is welcomed by a fly-pass of green, red, blue and yellow doves. They are real doves which have been plunged, quite painlessly, into vats of vegetable dye. There are more surprises in store: a magnificent chandelier hangs outside the house; the boundaries are marked by notices announcing 'Anyone throwing stones at this notice will be prosecuted'; a perfectly respectable statue is half-submerged in a lily pond; the swimming pool appears to have been made into a small crenellated castle; and a folly stands on top of a hill, a curious memorial to a twenty-first birthday present request for a horse.

The house and some of the parkland belonged to the thirties eccentric Lord Berners, immortalized by Nancy Mitford in *The Pursuit of Love* as Lord Merlin. Had she accurately described some of the garden at Faringdon House, had she simply written about the real thing, her novel might have appeared far-fetched, so instead she made believe that the reality was make-believe, and wrote: 'A marble folly on a nearby hill was topped with a gold angel which blew a trumpet every evening at the hour of Lord Merlin's birth.... Such a man was bound to become a sort of legend to the bluff Cotswold squires among whom he lived... [around the entrance of the house there was] a flock of multi-coloured pigeons tumbling about like a cloud of confetti in the sky.'

Lord Berners' eccentricity was aided and abetted by Robert Heber Percy, to whom he left the whole estate, lock, stock and barrel of tricks. In 1986, a year before his death, Robert Heber Percy spent one mellow autumn day showing me around his garden. He was so frail he could barely make his way down the small flight of steps at the front of his house. However, he insisted on driving around the garden which is very much his creation, his masterpiece. He steered haphazardly through flower beds, across manicured lawns and fields and along pastoral walks in a vehicle which might once have posed as a Morris van but by then bore a closer resemblance to a compost heap on wheels.

'The doves were Lord Berners' idea. He read about dyeing doves in a Chinese book. They should have whistles on their wings, too, but we never got round to that. We thought up some of the ideas together but I always did them,' said Robert Heber Percy, narrowly missing a small pyramid-shaped tombstone inscribed with the words: 'Towser – a short life but a gay one'.

Along the edge of the gravel sweep at the front of the house there is a line of stately urns which must once have dripped with gaudy nineteenth-century planting. Now they drip with plastic greenery. There was no need for the plastic because Robert Heber Percy could have called for real plants from any one of the talented gardeners around his estate. But there was something contrary about a great deal of his humour. A stone's throw from the gentle Georgian south face of Faringdon House, where jasmine and magnolia lean in abundance against the walls, past some fine old beech trees, there is a well-appointed Georgian orangery full of mouldering ancestral oils and great gilt mirrors. The orangery doors open on to a wide flagged terrace which sprouts all kinds of primulas in early summer, and to either side of the terrace there are inviting stone benches. At the centre of the terrace a half-submerged statue of a Victorian general gazes moodily out from the centre of a lily pond. 'Someone came to me and said, "Did you know you've got my great grandfather in the lily pond?" That was how I found out it was General Havelock. I found him in the chapel, and there was nowhere else to put him.' Which is a feeble excuse for ducking a general, because Faringdon estate rolls for a thousand acres or so.

The first well-recorded house on this estate was Elizabethan, although little is said of the gardens then. But then Faringdon was taken over by the poet laureate, magistrate and Berkshire militiaman Henry Pye, of whom Sir Walter Scott said, 'The poetical Pye was respectable in everything but his poetry.' Pye's architectural taste appears to have been more acceptable than his poetry, assuming, as most do, that he arranged for the building of the present 'neat villa' with a park and lake instead of the former large Elizabethan manor. The down-trading was necessary in order to get by on the dwindling resources of the estate. Resources dwindled still further when Pye was elected to parliament in 1784, and eventually Faringdon was sold on to the Cunards and then to Lord Berners.

Robert Heber Percy made the gardens at Faringdon as peculiar as Lord Berners made the house, where a life-size nodding-head dog stands incongruously in the marble-floored hall. A horse once joined guests for

THE
ORANGERY
AND THE
POOL,
GENERAL
HAVELOCK'S
WATERY
GRAVE

71

ABOVE THE CHANGING ROOM

LEFT THE CHANGING ROOM FLOOR, INLAID WITH PENNIES

tea in the small drawing room, a crooked chest of drawers is set beneath a Salvador Dali painting, a Rousseauesque jungle *trompe l'œil* covers one of the bathroom walls, a glass four-poster graces one of the bedrooms, and a framed notice on the front door reads, 'It is requested that all hats be removed'.

The garden tour continued as Robert Heber Percy aimed the van towards the centre of an old box hedge, narrowly missed it and coasted through to a patch of gravel beneath a crenellated swimming pool. The pool itself – solar-heated – sits in its own tiny castle complete with a turret which is the changing room, with a floor inlaid with old pennies – 'Well we had to put something on the floor.' On top of the turret there is a crowned bust. Two gigantic stone wyverns, strange heraldic two-legged dragon creatures first created for Queen Elizabeth I, leer over the side of the pool. Robert Heber Percy found them in Cornwall and decided he simply had to have them. For some people impulse buys are to do with silk frocks, but for Robert Heber Percy impulse buying was more to do with hard landscaping.

'I had to have a pool there because otherwise there was a great flight of steps up from the orangery with nothing but a fall on the other side. So I decided to put a swimming pool there. I put a lot of work into it. I thought it out carefully. So many people give so little

thought to swimming pools which can be such ugly things. It just had to be crenellated; it would have been so dull without that.'

The car careered off, its left flank dragging through a border of frilly-flowered *Hydrangea macrophylla* 'Serrata', roared down one steep and slippery track past a pool with a centrepiece of a great stone urn, and limped up the other side past views of the eighteenth-century landscaped park, complete with outsize stone urns, specimen trees, lakes and a bridge-spanned valley. Amid such grandeur a coach and four would seem a more fitting form of transport than Robert Heber Percy's alleged car, which behaved as if it would never make the top of the slope, grinding and slithering up the hill. At last we made it to the start of an alley of monkey puzzle trees leading to a stone monolith. This marks the spot where Lord Berners' ashes are scattered – or is he buried here? Robert Heber Percy appeared unable to make up his mind, and muttered darkly about 'the planners'. There is no inscription but Robert Heber Percy felt the stone ought to read:

HERE LIES LORD BERNERS,
ONE OF THE LEARNERS,
HIS GREAT LOVE OF LEARNING
MAY EARN HIM A BURNING
BUT PRAISE BE TO THE LORD
HE SELDOM WAS BORED.

Faringdon boasts another other-worldly oddity:

one area, not so far from the house, is said to be haunted by the murdered elder son of one of the generations of Pyes who lived at Faringdon. The story goes that his wicked stepmother plotted his death with the murder of the captain of the boy's ship while he was a serving midshipman. His head was blown off by a cannonball in what was said to be a skirmish with an enemy ship, but he still came back to Faringdon to scare his stepmother.

THERE'S A LADY SITS LONELY
   IN BOWER AND HALL
HER PAGES AND HANDMAIDENS
   COME TO HER CALL
'NOW HASTE YE MY MAIDENS, HASTE AND SEE
NOW HE SITS THERE AND GLOW'RS
   WITH HIS HEAD ON HIS KNEE.'

As if to balance out this ghostly part of the estate there is the Angel Walk, an avenue of trees where a small statue of an angel used to perch on a branch until it was stolen by some godless creature; but the walk retains its name.

A couple of weathered red-brick lodges appeared on the horizon at the end of the monkey puzzle alley, all delightfully neat and surrounded by carefully tended cottage gardens. Through one of the windows a fox could be seen settled into a comfy floral armchair reading a copy of the *Faringdon Standard*. It was – and still is – a *trompe l'œil* by Roy Hobdell, commissioned because 'A gamekeeper called Mr Fox lives there.'

Eccentric Gardens

After a brief disagreement with a wall the car span off into a field, crashing from hummock to bump like a Thelwell pony, past glorious views of undulating Oxfordshire, the Downs in the distance, past the fishpond that was transformed into a lake in 1800, reflecting dazzling yellow gold beeches, to a Second World War pillbox decorated by what Robert Heber Percy called his 'Cleopatra statue'. Others may know it as 'Egypt'. 'I bought this for £10 after the war from that glass place which burned down [the Crystal Palace]. We stuck it on top of this bunker thing built to surprise Germans during the war [a pillbox]. We set off at four a.m. with a tractor and drove to London to pick up the statue. But when we were coming back we stopped at every pub on the way. It was quite awkward because the statue kept wobbling and so we couldn't go round corners. That was quite a night.'

One of Egypt's sisters from the Crystal Palace muses at the end of a tree-lined avenue. This is probably Greece. The final stop on the motorized garden tour was the folly which stands on a pine-planted hillock just outside Faringdon. It is a noble brick building with a large windowed room at the top with views up and down the Thames valley. It can be seen from miles away. 'Lord Berners gave me this folly for my twenty-first birthday,' he says, waving at a 140-foot high brick edifice.

'Goodness how lovely.'

'No it wasn't. I wanted a horse.'

'Ah. What happens in the belvedere room at the top of the folly?'

'Lord Berners had a very good idea. He wanted to put a grand piano up there, one of those ones which plays automatically. And he wanted to be stuffed and put behind it as if he were playing it. You know, like Bentham. But I funked it – I never did it.'

'Why?'

'Because it's quite difficult to get a grand piano up there.'

In 1935, when Lord Berners started to build young Robert the folly (which is after all no worse an inspiration than building a Grecian temple for pigs, as happened at Fyling Hall in Yorkshire, or a temple for tortoises, as happened at Wooton House in Surrey) some townsfolk spent the summer being rude about it and trying to stop the work. Some wrote unfriendly letters about it to the local newspaper; some complained that it blocked their view of nothing in particular but that they didn't like it anyway; and one or two said it was an eyesore and should be pulled down. Friends of Lord Berners and Robert Heber Percy mischievously tried stirring furies still further by writing under pseudonyms to the local paper saying that they had heard the folly would include a foghorn

THE
TRANQUILLITY
OF THE LAKE
DISTURBED
ONLY BY THE
OCCASIONAL
DYED DOVE

Eccentric Gardens

THE FOLLY THAT LORD BERNERS BUILT

and lighthouse beam. (Faringdon is about as far inland as you can get in the British Isles.) But the folly was built and became a much-loved part of the landscape, causing a local pub to be named after it. And in 1985, with a neat twist of irony, Robert Heber Percy gave the folly to the town of Faringdon with a small trust fund for its upkeep. And, having restored Faringdon Folly itself after a few years of neglect he replanted 500 Scots pines around it so the hillock would be just right, just as Lord Berners planned it. 'This will be my last gesture,' he said.

And that was the last time I saw him. In the autumn of 1987 Robert Heber Percy, died and left Faringdon House and garden to his only granddaughter, Sofka Zinovieff, who, at the time, was in the middle of her PhD in Greek social anthropology at Cambridge University when she was given the completely unexpected news about her inheritance. Sofka Zinovieff, whose family on her father's side left Russia during the Revolution, seems to be shaping up nicely to her new responsibilities: Lord Merlin, alias Berners, used to irritate the local huntin', shootin' and fishin' community by keeping whippets with diamond collars. In real life Lord Berners kept dalmatians with diamond collars. Sofka Zinovieff on the other hand dyed her mother's whippets mauve, and she jokes that it might have been a good idea to have dyed her own hair to match that of the dogs.

She is going to continue to dye the doves and keep the garden's strangeness as it is. It has been a while since Faringdon looked so cheery and spruce, but in the tidying up operation, the trimming and the clearing it does not appear to have lost any of its magic. The Angel Walk has been replaced with young trees: laburnum, winter-flowering cherry and crataegus, and one day, perhaps, even the angel may be replaced. Sofka Zinovieff has breathed life into the house. It is summer. The doors are open and from the front door, you can see past sets of double doors to the parkland beyond the formal gardens. Through to the back of the house, and on a stone terrace tea is being taken. In the fields below, Sofka Zinovieff's newly married brother and his bride run and shout and throw a huge blue kite into the air. About half a mile away there is a Swiss cottage-style summer house beside the lake. They – she and her brothers and mother and friends – swim in the lake despite local talk of large-fanged pike lurking in the muddy bottom. She boats about on the lake too, and loves it and the water lilies that dot the surface.

Here Sofka Zinovieff has summer parties at night with a waterfall rushing out from under the summer house. Here still hangs another notice left by Lord Berners and Robert Heber Percy:

Eccentric Gardens

THE KISS OF THE SUN FOR PARDON
THE SONG OF THE BIRDS FOR MIRTH
ONE IS NEARER TO GOD'S HEART IN A GARDEN
THAN ANYWHERE ELSE ON THE EARTH.

Perhaps she'll add her own brand of eccentricity to the garden; this is still early days. She never talked to her grandfather about it or about his expectations of her, but she is alive with plans to add to the garden, to plant and to replace plants and shrubs and trees which have begun to go over. It has to be done without any pointers or guidelines from those who created the grounds. Robert Heber Percy couldn't or wouldn't outline any of his intentions or ambitions for his garden. She has been left to work out this paradise for herself. It is the stuff of fairy tales.

West Wycombe Park is or was, in a sense, the stuff of nightmares. At least that is how it must have seemed to those who heard the rumours about Goings-On at West Wycombe during the eighteenth century, under the dashing second Sir Francis Dashwood of Hell Fire fame. The present Sir Francis Dashwood, descendant of the Hell Fire Sir Francis, and author of a scholarly book about his family, has restored his ancestor's magnificent park set on the edge of the Chilterns at West Wycombe in Buckinghamshire. He has also gone some way towards restoring the reputation of his forebear, seriously sullied by Horace Walpole who wrote terrible things about the eighteenth century Sir Francis and his activities. Which is why the brisk and businesslike present Sir Francis is anxious to point out that his newly restored and rather erotic Venus garden is only one small and relatively unimportant part of this historically significant park, and that his ancestor was not as reprobate as many of us would like to believe.

The garden, not far from the lake in front of the house, is made up of an oval temple to the goddess set on a mount with a path running down either side. The temple and setting are supposed to represent the goddess, and the two paths her open legs. Today the paths are not obvious, but until recently none of this garden was obvious, having been overgrown since the last century.

It was, appropriately, a labour of love to resurrect the goddess's temple and her garden, built originally in 1739, probably by a draughtsman named Donowell (who was dismissed around 1764 for reasons which are not clear), before Sir Francis's extensive alterations to West Wycombe House were completed. The present Sir Francis, his wife Marcella, their children and weekend guests who could be roped into a little manual labour spent three winters digging and clearing the area. With attention to detail and historical

THE PRESENT
SIR FRANCIS AND
FRIEND

accuracy Sir Francis researched the Temple of Venus garden, which had been removed in the nineteenth century, using original architectural drawings, now framed on his study wall, and the many eighteenth-century paintings of the garden dotted around the house upstairs and down.

Sir Francis explains the erotic symbolism between bellows to the dogs, who romp happily around the park and their master's feet. 'This is the only oval temple in Britain – it's oval because it's symbolic of Venus. The Temple of Venus – this one was designed by Quinlan Terry to look like the original – is set on Venus's mount, and the two paths down either side of the mound represent her legs and this is Venus's parlour, which represents Venus's anatomy – well,

you can imagine what that is. In the paintings you see much more of the paths – the legs – delineated,' says the present Sir Francis.

The Mount is a small curved, flint façade set into the bottom of the grass mound on which the temple stands. There are two niches which once held urns, one to Potiphar's wife and the other to the Ephesian ladies who were the heroines of a slightly obscene Roman novel. 'It was a joke,' says Sir Francis. In between the urns there is an oval orifice which runs into a tiny brick-lined quintessentially feminine oval cavity.

Sir Francis loves his park, his house and his ancestor, and as far as he is concerned there is but one blot on this otherwise perfect landscape: evidence of activity by the early nineteenth century landscaper Humphry Repton, who was responsible for the few bits and pieces which irritate Sir Francis about West Wycombe. 'Repton was hopeless here in my view. He was appointed by Sir John Dashwood King, who was the son of Sir Francis's half-brother who married Milton's sister's great granddaughter, so he was a very pious and upright MP who was obviously shocked by his father's half-brother's activities here and proceeded to remove everything. That's St Crispin's,' says Sir Francis, waving at a church-like building in the distance beyond the lake. 'It had a spire on it which

Repton took off because he said it was ridiculous having a building which was designed like a church and calling it St Crispin's when in fact it was occupied by a shoemaker. But what was ridiculous was Repton – he insisted on having the spire taken off. I think the problem was that Repton was overwhelmed by West Wycombe. Unlike most of his other projects there wasn't much for him to do here because it had all been done already, so all he could think of doing was to clear a few things.' Sir Francis knows his onions and rattles off names and dates without a break in his stride.

Repton's spirit when writing about West Wycombe was wonderfully confident. He was particularly keen on the lake and in 'Observations' (1805) he wrote, 'The water at West Wycombe, from the brilliancy of its colour, the variety of its shores, the different courses of its channel, and the number of its wooded islands, possessed a degree of pleasing intimacy which I have rarely seen in artificial pools or rivers; there appears to be only one improvement necessary to give it all the variety of which it is capable. The glassy surface of a still calm lake, however delightful, is not more interesting than the lively brook rippling over a rocky bed; but when the latter is compared with a narrow stagnant creek, it must have a decided prefer–ence...' and he goes on to suggest a little cleverly

placed rock in the lake near the house so the brook effect could be seen easily.

These suggestions do not impress Sir Francis. 'All he did here was to remove masses of statues – he took about twenty-eight statues from this temple – and he also seems to have been responsible for taking away statues of Venus and Mercury which I've just put back. He and Sir John Dashwood King appear to have done this in 1796. The temple appears to have gone in around 1807. In the nineteenth century they might have been shocked by all the naked statues I suppose. There was a reversal then, after the eighteenth century. I don't know what all the twenty-eight statues originally were but it says in the lists of furniture of 1781 "in different positions" so they might have been slightly erotic.'

When it came to replacing the goddess herself in her temple, Sir Francis found a copy Venus de Milo rather than a Venus de Medici who originally lived here. 'The Venus de Milo is not really lifelike enough whereas the Venus de Medici is a full woman, but unfortunately I couldn't find a fibreglass Venus de Medici, and a stone one would have cost too much.'

The only well-documented statues are Venus herself in the temple and one of Mercury just in front of her mound and, having restored them, Sir Francis is thinking about restoring the sculpture of Leda being

raped by the swan which adorned the top of the original temple. But even getting to this stage has cost the Dashwood family blood, sweat and cash. 'The whole area here was stinging nettles and bog,' says Sir Francis, waving at the clipped grass around the Venus garden. 'We knew from paintings that the temple had been here, but the area was covered with ash suckers, quite big ones. We had them cut down but there was a lot of elder as well and so every weekend if any of our children were here or friends they all came along and gave a hand – but I must say my wife did a fantastic amount of the digging. Eighteen inches down we found the original base of the temple and some brick tiles which formed the base and that was how we discovered that it was oval. The temple was the most painted scene here in the eighteenth century so we decided to put it back. Sir Francis never wrote anything about the Venus garden but he was very keen on the female form.'

He was also pretty keen on West Wycombe itself which, mostly thanks to him, boasts a total of twelve temples, a lake contoured into the shape of a swan, tree-lined walks, and magnificent views across the Wye valley. Working drawings of the garden have been uncovered in the attics, but one of the most vivid documents is a detailed map dated 1752. That and a much larger map of the estate as a whole in 1767 hang

VENUS'S MOUNT AND TEMPLE RESTORED TO GLORY AT WEST
WYCOMBE IN BUCKINGHAMSHIRE. THE ORIGINAL TEMPLE WAS
TOPPED WITH A STATUE OF LEDA AND THE SWAN

in Sir Francis's bedroom, along with paintings of the landscapes by William Hannan and his apprentices.

Like the first Sir Francis, the present holder of the name and title works in the City. This one has tremendous respect for his ancestor, and his accounts of the first Sir Francis suggest the antithesis of the wild and wicked image that has grown up about the eighteenth-century Sir Francis. The aura of scandal around the first Sir Francis, hyped by political adversaries, was largely due to his activities in political opposition. When gossip began to circulate about the goings-on in his 'Hell Fire Club', aka 'Monks of Medmenham', aka 'The Knights of St Francis of Wycombe', the scandal waxed and grew. Tales about orgies and quasi-religious ceremonies were bread and wine to those who disliked Sir Francis.

Whether or not the first Sir Francis was a wild one, the fact remains that he threw himself into the creation of this now magnificent estate having bought out his brother's share for £15,000 in 1698. Some of the inspiration for the estate came from Sir Francis's grand tours when he travelled to Italy, France, Germany, Russia, Greece and Asia Minor, which were not always the sober paintin', learnin' and writin' affairs of less imaginative noblemen. His many adventures included gate-crashing scourging ceremonies at the Sistine Chapel during Holy Week and then going to work with a horsewhip as soon as the lights were put out.

The present Sir Francis has thrown himself into restoring the park, with the help of the late Lanning Roper, Russell Page, John Sale and the National Trust, which now owns the park and the house. He has added such inspired touches as buying a defunct fibre glass equine statue from Pinewood to grace the brow of the tree-lined avenue (restored by him to its eighteenth-century splendour) and commissioning a cricket pavilion cunningly designed by Quinlan Terry to look like a temple. He is also planning to add a powerful waterspout which will, he hopes, leap into the air *à la* Chatsworth.

Raw ambition and competitiveness has always played a part in the formation of the English landscape: if Capability Brown had wiped out a landowner's seventeenth-century Italianate terraces in favour of the natural look then one had to do the same – even better and add more lakes, more deer parks and move more hills. Otherwise how could one have held up one's head in society? Sir Francis has no need to compete, but he is snooty, at the moment, about Castle Howard's Temple of the Winds. 'I've no idea why it is called the Temple of the Winds because it is totally incorrect – it has only four sides whereas there were eight classical winds. That's why this temple,' he says, waving at an eight-sided flint and stucco

THE EQUINE STATUE ON
THE HORIZON CAME FROM
PINEWOOD FILM STUDIOS

construction at the back of the house, 'is called the Temple of the Winds. Sir Francis was very well read; he made sure that his classical references were correct. People forget that.' And his was, possibly, the first temple based on an antique model to have been built in this country. This one, a copy of the third-century Roman temple at Athens and probably the work of Nicholas Revett, was finished in 1759, whereas James Stuart's Temples of the Winds at Mount Stewart and Shugborough came a few years later.

Now, despite the despised Repton, West Wycombe is moving towards its original glory, naughty bits, eccentricities and all, which inspired Benjamin Franklin, a regular guest of Hell Fire Sir Francis, to write in 1773: 'I am in this house as much at my ease as if it were my own: and the gardens are paradise.'

Beastly Backyards

Hull city is a fine old port, and the pride of the city, the longest single-span suspension bridge in the world, has grace, beauty and style. The route to Fred Button's garden in Hull, on the other hand, is not promising. The outskirts of the city are an urban sprawl. That cosmetic lick of wealth which sometimes cheers up a city is nowhere to be found. Fred Button's garden is tucked away in a crescent of post-war semi-detached houses immediately behind the city football ground. There is a privet hedge and not much else at the front but at the back there is another world. It is Fred's own paradise of parrots, pools, water spouts and fountains, statues and pergolas. The garden is a quarter of an acre at most, but into that Fred has packed everything including a palm tree.

When Fred Button left Hull University where he was a porter – not any old porter but a porter chosen by Philip Larkin, the poet, after a forty-minute interview – Fred's colleagues and friends clubbed together to buy him some parrots.

There are small parrots, big parrots, singing parrots, parrots on perches, free-wheeling parrots. They are brought into the house during the winter but in the summer the garden is alive with the birds swinging from tree to tree. Inspiration for this parrot mania came from his wife Kathleen, whose dowry included a parrot called, quite properly, Polly. Polly was a Yellowhead Amazon and when Polly died, when she no longer whistled at the workmen in the street, when she no longer chatted to Fred and Kathleen, there was much mourning and much searching of souls over whether to find another parrot. They decided not to, and instead Fred bought a plastic parrot to put in Polly's cage, so starting a quest to fill his garden with parrots.

The parrots came from every source. Many of the parrots to be found in shops were too expensive, or they weren't plastic, in which case they couldn't withstand the weather out of doors and so there was no point in having more than a handful of them. The Buttons relied on gifts, on presents of plastic parrots from thoughtful friends, and bought only a few.

The pergola just outside their back door is alive with parrots, small and large, dangling from the beams; the arch at the end of the garden towards the compost heap boasts a strange head carved from a coconut. There are a couple more of these sinister voodooesque ornaments near the house.

Like the ornaments in the garden, the trees too are peculiar. Fred Button has discovered how to make standard lavatera, in the same way that you make

Eccentric Gardens

WHO WOULDN'T LOOK
GLOOMY WITH THOSE TWO
SHARING ONE'S PERCH

SOUTH SEAS
DECORATION ON
HUMBERSIDE

PART OF FRED
BUTTON'S
EXOTIC BACK
GARDEN IN
HULL

91

standard fuchsias, by pulling off the side shoots. While many other trees are dull and silent through the winter, Fred Button's semi-hardy 'trees' sometimes stay covered in grey-green foliage, and during most of the spring and summer they are covered in pink mallow flowers which give a suitably exotic backdrop for the birds.

Soon after Fred Button took over the garden (it had belonged to Kathleen's father until he died) he heard about Hull City Council's 'Hull in Bloom' contest. 'I thought about all those people in the area like managing directors for whom money is no object and thought it would never be worth entering my garden. But then I thought I'd have a go anyway,' said Fred, whose front room is a shrine to parrots and gardens, with the more delicate model parrots hanging around the room and photographs of the garden at various stages during the year. So he thought up new ways of adding interest and cheer to the garden without it costing too much. He built a series of little pools and water spouts. One fountain formed an umbrella of water over a statue of a boy who stands guard over a pool of fat goldfish. Finally there were a total of six water spouts or fountains trickling through his garden, and one small problem. An ugly box of a transformer pumped the water around the garden but created an eyesore. So to hide it Fred built a casing in the shape of a dolls' house around the transformer.

He also found one or two old garden ornaments, like a long-forgotten bird bath buried in the compost heap. 'I found it while Kathleen was out shopping. It was broken so I mended it, painted it and put it up in the centre of the garden. She had a shock when she came back. She said she hadn't seen it for forty years since she was a child growing up in this house and garden – and she'd always wondered what had happened to it.' An ornate concrete dolphin was found, too, and this Fred Button cleaned down and painted in vivid colours. He likes bright things. A windmill, a frog on a mushroom, a gnome and a tortoise all received the same bright colour treatment. 'They were dull grey stone. They needed a lick of paint to make them look interesting.'

Someone gave Fred and Kathleen a plastic penguin which is bird-like and begins with a 'p', even if it isn't quite a parrot. Then Fred Button found a type of sealed-beam American headlight which could be adapted to make floating lights for the pools, so the garden was given life at night as well as by day.

As the garden took shape, Kathleen watched from her station in the doorway of the shed at the end of the garden. Sitting amongst the pots, the spades, the rakes and the forks she soaked up the sun and added her suggestions to the garden. One day, on one of their

WATER SPOUTS
AND TINY
FOUNTAINS
ABOUND

THE BUTTONS
PICTURED IN THEIR
SHED/CHALET

Fred felt a Swiss chalet would look cheery at the bottom of the garden instead of the old shed. The shed was installed and ornament added. Tyrolean decorations were stuck to the front of the hut to make a fringe of wood carving along the edge of the roof, while inside curtains were hung in the window and carpet fitted over the simple wooden floor. Antlers were strapped above the door and, up the wooden wall on the outside of the shed, gold cherubs were encouraged to fly alongside a model of a faintly nautical-looking type smoking a pipe. A boomerang was added to the decoration, which, although not an immediately obvious way to adorn a Swiss chalet, was liked by Fred Button and that is reason enough.

'I'm a home bird. I'm not bothered about travelling or seeing other people's gardens. I do things to please myself. I'm not bothered what other people think. My neighbours like the garden. In some ways I'm crazy, I am.' Not so crazy. He has won various prizes in the 'Hull in Bloom' competition, and quite rightly, because at the height of the season this garden is a riot of plant colour. Swathes of nemesia, marigolds, wallflowers, pansies, bachelor's buttons, bergenia, salvia, Livingstone daisies, geraniums and verbena huddle together amongst alpine and exotic features to create a landscape quite unlike anything else.

Now Fred and Kathleen can admire their displays

weekend tours of local garden centres searching for new ornaments Fred took Kathleen to a spanking new garden shed in a garden supplies shop. 'I shall buy you this,' he said, although Fred Button being Fred Button, a new shed alone was not enough. 'And I shall turn it into a Swiss chalet for you.'

THE GARDEN SHED
REINCARNATED

from the comfort of their luxury Swiss-chalet-cum-tool-shed. There are a few tools round the back, but for the most part the chalet is an inviting den, with an electric fire, a tea-making machine, tea towels pinned to the walls, two striped garden chairs, a table and a cuckoo clock. On Saturdays, late in the football season when the crowds in the stadium roar and shout, Fred and Kathleen Button relax in a Tyrolean landscape a world away from their neighbours – and from almost anything else to do with the north-eastern coast of Britain in the late twentieth century.

A few hundred miles north of Fred Button's garden, still on the coastline, is the county of Northumberland, birthplace of England's most famous landscape designer, Lancelot 'Capability' Brown. He was born in 1716 at Kirkharle, started work at sixteen as a lowly gardener to Sir William Lorraine, and rapidly moved on to greater things and grander people. John Fairnington was born two centuries later in the same county, and, unlike Capability, who created dozens of landscapes for his patrons, made just one garden. That garden is beginning to acquire as much notoriety as Capability Brown's landscapes attracted fame and accolades.

The history of the garden, which was made by one family and their tiny Northumberland community,

Branxton village, for an only son, is a story told by John Fairnington Junior, the nephew of the man who started it, John Fairnington Senior. John Fairnington Junior runs his late uncle's joinery business and cares for the garden left behind.

In 1935 John Fairnington, a fifty-three-year-old master joiner whose family had been in the joinery business for two hundred years, was blessed with his only child, Edwin. Edwin was slightly handicapped, and so when his doting father retired at the age of eighty he started sketching working drawings of a life-size model of a panda bear, which he planned to build outside in the garden to encourage Edwin to play outside their post-war home. He scribbled a drawing of the panda – from a book, never having been beyond these shores or indeed to a zoo – and made the creature from a chicken-wire base, stuffed with waste paper and coated with concrete. The panda delighted Edwin, and so the demand for animals was created and John Fairnington, helped by some kind neighbours, a Mr William Collins and then a Mr James Beveridge, threw himself into turning the humble back garden from which one can see the battlefield of Flodden into a menagerie, a cement menagerie.

Camels, a giraffe, a life-sized cart horse complete with real tack appeared like magic before Edwin's eyes. Every size and shape of animal, from rabbits and

THE BEASTS WERE MADE TO
ENTERTAIN AN ONLY CHILD

mice to a unicorn, long-horned cattle, shepherds and sheep, hippo and buffalo were created. Characters like the minister (John Fairnington was a superintendent and a Sunday school teacher) and a Buddha growing out of the top of an old tree stump were added to the garden year by year. A wishing well appeared and more animals including a monarch of the glen, a three dimensional version of the Landseer painting added character. John Fairnington then purchased part of the next-door garden and continued his work for Edwin, extending the child's paradise, the grandest most glorious boy's playing field in Northumberland. A horseman sat waiting for battle. Sometimes the Fairningtons painted him blue and called him a Scotsman; sometimes they painted him red and called him an Englishman.

Today the garden is a little shabby, a bit ragged around the edges, but the crazy joy of it lives on.

All around the garden are labels and poems and sayings: the summerhouse at one corner of the garden bears a plaque which reads: 'Life is like a flowing stream. Once passed it can never return.' A Moffat ram stands on a stone pedestal with the caption:

THE MOFFAT RAM DOES STAND AND STARE
AT ALL THE PEOPLE IN THE SQUARE.

And here is how the concrete cow is celebrated:

THIS HAS BEEN A FAMOUS COO

NOT MUCH ROOM FOR PLANTS IN THIS
HIGHLY POPULATED GARDEN, SO THE ODD
CONIFER AND HEATHER HAS TO SUFFICE

WOULD LANDSEER
HAVE APPROVED?

TEN CALVES IN TWELVE SHORT YEARS
HER CARCASS SHOULD MAKE
  A SAVOURY STEW
HERE IS NO CAUSE FOR TEARS.

Then there's the poem:

IN THE GARDEN GROW
FAR MORE THAN HERBS OR FLOWERS
KIND THOUGHTS
CONTENTMENT
PEACE OF MIND
AND JOY FOR MANY HOURS.

And at the far end of the garden there is a platform from which to view the gardens to one side and the other. In the distance is the boundary of Scotland and England.

In between the life-size models of people and of animals John Fairnington built a hut where visitors could sit and admire the garden, a fish pond, an ornamental wind vane and a network of paths around all the models. This eruption of fantastic art sits especially strangely in the countryside of Northumberland: wild, splendid moorland, and a wilder coast with magnificent wind-torn beaches, make an odd setting for an animal garden.

Help in making this garden came from unexpected quarters. The local butcher saved sheep's skulls, and sometimes John and local villagers found other animal skulls up on the moors on which an anatomically accurate head could be built, even if the body was a little out of proportion. They went in for accuracy, wherever they could, checking and double-checking the animals they had never seen against pictures, photographs and the word of those who had seen the beast in question. Fairnington's wife, Edwin's mother, must have watched these developments with a slightly faint heart; she was a keen gardener and here, before her eyes, the scope for horticultural creativity and experiment was being severely limited. But rather

ABOVE SOME OF THE CEMENT PEOPLE WERE MODELLED ON VILLAGERS

LEFT POEMS AND SAYINGS ARE DOTTED AROUND THIS LANDSCAPE

EDWIN'S PLAYGROUND

than stop the building of this playground, Edwin's mother simply planted heathers and bedding in every inch left by the menagerie and the paths winding around the creatures.

When Edwin died, aged thirty-six, his father created a chalet-like memorial to him with marble imported specially from Italy. They called it Memory Corner. On the marble he embossed a smiling picture of the man who inspired this strange garden, where Lawrence of Arabia stands beside camels and elephants. When John Fairnington died, aged ninety-nine, the garden faced death too. In his will he left the garden to six charities. Confronted with the problem of how six charities could share one garden, business-men were sent to Northumberland to inspect the lie of the land and come up with a solution. They decided that it was a garden of no importance, that this was 'crude art' and that it should be destroyed and the land sold. Well that is how the Fairnington family tell the story. The family was hurt by what they saw as a snub to an extraordinary work of love and devotion. So John Fairnington Junior, scraped together some money, bought the garden and now runs it with the help of friends. 'Some folk think my uncle a little bit crazy but I don't know. He gave a lot of pleasure to a lot of people. People come from all over the world to see this garden now.'

THE DEAD ARE
REMEMBERED
HERE WHERE,
ONCE, EDWIN
PLAYED

103

Eccentric Gardens

Sir Winston Churchill guards the entrance to the garden. No fee is demanded but a collection box is a polite reminder that a cement menagerie cannot live on air. John Fairnington refuses to introduce a compulsory charge partly because of one of the inscriptions:

THE NICEST THING ABOUT THIS LIFE
IT ALWAYS SEEMS TO ME
IS WHEN SO MUCH COSTS OF SO MUCH
THE LOVELIEST THINGS ARE FREE.

The animals that roam the Fairnington's garden have little connection with reality, apart from the odd skull. But there are some gardens where the ornament comes, in part, from the remains of real animals. At West Dean Gardens in Sussex, for instance, the floor of Harold Peto's pavilion is made from a pretty cartwheel pattern of flints and horses' molars. This unexpected beastliness makes a startling contrast to the homely atmosphere of the rest of that part of the garden, some of which was designed by Gertrude Jekyll.

Banwell Cave gardens in Avon are yet more beastly. It is a garden born of bones, a garden of follies, strangeness and of dreams, Victorian dreams of Druids and cosy weirdness, seen from the warmth of a Victorian parlour once inhabited by the nineteenth century Bishop of Bath and Wells, Bishop Law. Today his country retreat is owned by two active families with dogs and cars, and so it can't have quite the atmosphere of the time when the palæontologist Bishop roamed the hill like the hero of some Gothic novel. Then this steep, misty, forbidding hill was difficult to reach, and travellers had no way of knowing how fast they would be able to escape if the inhabitants on top of the hill proved hostile. And even with the two jolly families in residence here, the Haynes and the Sargents, even with the M5 curling snake-like around the bottom of Banwell Hill, sending a great roar up to the top of it, the gardens have an odd atmosphere, considerably improved during spring when the hillside shows off by sprouting great sweeps of snowdrops, followed by carpets of primroses and daffodils and then of bluebells.

These gardens were built around thousands of bones, many of which are neatly stacked and pleasingly arranged in a great natural cavern under the steep, knee-like hill which falls away on three sides to the Avon countryside below. To reach the bone cave you follow such a sweet, innocent path, with lawn and beds on either side, that it is difficult to prepare for what is in store. Down stone steps to a locked metal gate which creaks open in the regulation Hammer-horror-movie style to a dingy cave. It is high, probably fifteen feet at the highest point, with the rock

FIDO'S PARADISE, PART OF THE BONE PATTERN
AT BANWELL CAVE GARDENS IN AVON

interior reaching down to the cave floor, where tiny passages can just be made out in the dim torchlight. Around the walls of some of the interior there are the pretty patterns of bones, the work of William Beard, a local man who helped Bishop Law explore caves and felt it improper to leave the bones as they had been found, in heaps. The bones are so well matched for size that it is possible to admire the design for a moment before remembering what it is made of. Perhaps the attractive design was the inspiration which caused the good Bishop to build a bone temple higher up the hill. For those who do not suffer from claustrophobia there are, I am reliably informed, some spectacular sights further on inside the network of caves which runs underneath the hill: the Ruby Cave, which looks 'like the intestines on a butchers slab', says one of the current owners of the caves, Yvonne Sargent; and a frozen river grotto. Yvonne Sargent is claustrophobic. She gets through the tiny crevices to these subterranean treasures by making the experts go first, closing her eyes, and then crawling through.

On the land above the caves there are the more accessible sights: a 'Victorian Druids' Temple' (said by some to have been built by the Bishop on the site of a real Druids' worshipping place); a 'Neolithic burial mound' (there is nothing Neolithic about it: it is another manifestation of the Bishop's somewhat

unusual preoccupations); a pebble summer house with the remains of a small stone camel; and a stone tower or folly. This may have been built by the Bishop's son, Henry Law, who was the rector of Weston-super-Mare. He had helped with the gardens from the beginning. By the 1840s, when the tower was completed and the Bishop was nearing the end of his life, he appears to have gone a little potty, although there is no record whether the events were connected.

Bishop Law must have been fairly eccentric to begin with. Why else would a man of the cloth build a Druids' Temple, a funny almost semicircular little building with five pillared arches which stands at the foot of the Haynes's and Sargents's steep drive? There is a little pebble cornice on top of a table inside and an inscription which reads:

HERE, WHERE THE DRUIDS TROD
  IN TIME OF YORE
AND STAINED THEIR ALTARS WITH
  A VICTIM'S GORE
HERE, NOW, THE CHRISTIAN
  RANSOMED FROM ABOVE
ADORES A GOD OF MERCY AND OF LOVE.

Across the drive there is what appears to be the remains of a second, mirror-image 'temple'. Yvonne Sargent has a theory about the Druids' temples: 'I know why he built them. It was all because he wanted to find a way of turning people back to God. He would have William Beard tell how the bones came into the

ONCE THIS
COTTAGE
HOUSED
SUNDAY
SCHOOL
PICNICS
HOSTED BY
BISHOP LAW

DRUIDS' TEMPLE,
NINETEENTH-CENTURY STYLE

cave because of The Flood and how the Druids' religion came to an end because of their ungodly practices.'

Then there is a stalactite cave. Follow some of the strange rambling paths laid out by the Bishop, still visible thanks to small stone walls on either side of every path, and you reach this second cave, to one side of the house and a great deal higher than the first cave. The locked wooden door which is the entrance to this cave is found by plunging down perilously steep steps into this perilously deep site. Rumour has it that someone once stole some of the stalactites to sell to other, less well-endowed caves.

The owners are nurturing the landscape over the caves like their own, stripping away the brambles to reveal yet another extraordinary little once-thatched stone summer house, with lead and glass in the windows, where the Bishop used to take his Sunday school picnics and outings. The ruined cottages, which are dotted through the great wet tangled woods around the hill, are still strangled by magnificent ivies. Two flights of stone stairs in the gardens lead – nowhere. Clamber through the small paths cut deep into the scramble of undergrowth and you eventually reach the top of the hill, where there is a larger path running along the backbone of the hill past a vast iron water tank and a pair of ten-foot-high tufa gate posts.

From now on the path is marked out by smaller blocks of tufa, and up here, suddenly, the gardens seem less eerie; there is more light and air here than on the side of the hill which houses the temples and caves. Gradually the two families are clearing the area, although they will retain woods in a tidier, less brambly form.

Banwell Cave gardens are being restored by Yvonne and Ronald Sargent and Margaret and John Haynes. The families moved in soon after Margaret Haynes decided she wanted a nice old house for her and her husband to restore at their leisure. Somewhere pretty, any house so long as it had an attic. A friend told them he'd seen just the house. He said that they'd love Banwell. They did, so they joined forces with another family, the Sargents whom they'd met a couple of years earlier, and bought the house and the garden jointly. The property has no attic. But it does have lots of bones, curious outbuildings and an unusual history.

The caves were rediscovered in 1800 by a couple of miners searching for lead and calamine. They found nothing of any interest to themselves, and abandoned the project. But just down the hill a farmer called William Beard (nicknamed The Professor by the Bishop), who remembered childhood stories about bone-filled caves on the land, contacted the miners and asked for their help. The threesome returned to the hillside to continue excavations, and found a stalactite cave. In an attempt to make an easier access to that cave by burrowing horizontally into the hill at a lower level, they discovered a fissure about twenty feet long, which led into a smaller cave piled with the bones of long dead animals.

As soon as the caves were unearthed the Bishop, fascinated by news of the bone discovery, built himself a *cottage orné* (on the gloomier side of the hill) so that he could stay in close proximity to the bone finds. Then began the Bishop's work to landscape the ground around the caves so he could open the bone caves and the garden to the public. He did so, charging half a guinea a time to see bison bones and all manner of others – except horse and human – arranged in herringbone and basketweave patterns around the walls. William Beard was so thrilled by the discoveries that he gave up farming to search for more bones and to guide visitors around the Bishop's caves and gardens. The money made from these guided tours went to a local charity.

There is mystery all about this garden, not least about the origin of the bones. Even today there are thousands of bones, despite the fact that many were taken as trophies by Victorian visitors to the garden. But no one knows who put the bones in the caves in the first place, or why they put them there. One of the bones is being radio carbon-dated, and according to the man in charge of this lengthy operation, Andy Current, Curator of Quaternary Mammals at the Natural History Museum, some of the bones are about forty thousand years old. The bones tell of a time when huge bison, reindeer, the large brown bear and wolves lived in this area. He reckons the cave was not a place of sinister goings-on, where animals were ritually slaughtered, but a place where animals tended to drown or get trapped rather too regularly. The bones, or perhaps whole animals, appear to have come in through a hole now sealed over in the top of the cave. There are many bones left in the cave, others can be found in museums around the country and some have gone forever, carted off in the last century for bonemeal fertilizer.

Today the scrubby, overgrown garden in front of the house and in between the two caves is being smartened up, and the Haynes and the Sargents are busy planting comfortable Victorian shrubs like rhododendrons and azaleas. Every now and then they, like the Bishop, open the gardens and the caves to the public. But sometimes they tire of being responsible and domestic and they disappear into their caves with a candle, exploring deep down, crawling on their stomachs with a torch to light their way to more distant caves. It is no less than the Bishop himself once did.

THE TOWER,
AT THE
PINNACLE OF
BANWELL CAVE
GARDENS

Entertaining Gardens

Anita Roddick has always shared her garden, and encouraged others to join her and her family in enjoying it. It is a party garden, first and foremost, a garden in which people of every age and disposition can relax and celebrate. Anita is founder head of the Body Shop, one of Britain's most spectacularly successful green businesses, whose animal-friendly, environment-conscious potions, unctions and oils now fill the shelves of women and men around the world. Her garden in West Sussex is also one of the few places in which Anita can relax and revive herself. She designed it with the help of Julian Treyer-Evans, once an army officer and now a gentle-mannered garden designer to the rich and famous. Anita is especially keen on him because, in her words, 'He is not a prima donna. He is exciting to work with. Every time I go to see a movie like "The Draughtsman's Contract" I come back with new ideas and say, for instance, what can we do with sheets blowing? How can we add them to the garden? And of course nothing but bird shit gets in the sheets. But he listens and helps me with ideas.'

Anita had told Julian she wanted a magical garden, a garden with a sense of humour, a garden she could share. The ground was thick chalk, the area outside her house a steep hill, and so the bulldozers arrived. They scooped out a large chunk of the hill and put it in the next-door field having first scraped away all the field's topsoil, bar six inches, to put on the garden. Twenty ten ton loads of well rotted mushroom compost; four men and £10,000 had to be found to build the wall around the perimeter of the walled garden alone (Julian is vague about precise costs because this was such an enormous job it was difficult to give any definite estimate); Julian and a team of eight men and a foreman began work in October, finishing in April, at which point the planting began and went on until June. The planting got off to a fine start because they installed a complex and highly efficient automatic watering system to cover every inch of the soil, flower bed or lawn. During the night this system sniffs the air and soil to decide whether water is needed and then, if it is, waters the garden with a labyrinth of underground pipes, some perforated, snaking through the flower beds; some attached to small watering mushrooms dotted under the lawns and pushed skywards by water pressure; and some fifteen-inch tubes fitted with a spray on top which squirts water over a large area.

Within months of the first bulldozer arriving, the garden was ready for its first guests.

Anita Roddick has poured thousands of pounds as

ANNITA RODDICK'S NEIGHBOURING FARMER
AND HIS COWS LEANING OVER A SUSSEX WALL.
FIBREGLASS CAN BE VERY CONVINCING

well as great eruptions of her own inspiration into her four acres in order to give friends, relations and neighbours as much pleasure as herself. The garden reflects bundles of ideas, all novel, some odd. It rises heavenwards from the back of the house in irregular terraces, each level or terrace containing a garden – like the herb garden which also contains a barbecue. 'The barbecue area is brilliant. It is made with Provençal stone, and the yew hedges are flat almost like seats, and all of that part of the garden is planted with white daisies, my favourite flowers, huge pots of them.'

Wide sweeps of brick steps lead straight up from the house through the garden, with paths branching off on either side to disparate areas of the garden: to the wilder garden, for instance, or to the Japanese garden, a clever sculptural slot just outside one of the bathrooms in the house. The main steps make their first stop at an airy white-wire pavilion with table and chairs, then at a giant draughts board which looks like an enormous pink and white table cloth. It was going to be a chess board but Anita Roddick can't play chess so it's a draughts board instead. Finally the steps appear to rise into nothingness, except that on the horizon at the top of the garden there is a man sitting, chin in hand, elbow on knee with his back to you and to the house, gazing out across the Sussex downs. This is actually a statue, referred to by Anita Roddick

Eccentric Gardens

DRAUGHTS PROVED TOO MUCH
FOR THE DENTAL TECHNICIAN

as her 'dental technician'. 'He was modelled on a real dental technician although.... At the top of the garden there is such a marvellous vista of the downs that you just have to sit and look at it, and he's reinforcing that.'

Over the wall to one side of Anita Roddick's garden on one of the windier parts of the downs, a farmer leans thoughtfully on the stonework, gazing towards the house; three cows at his right hand are staring in the same direction. And when a new housekeeper arrived from New Zealand she spent the first few days thinking that the local farmer was suffering from paralysis. In fact this farmer is fibreglass, and so are the cows. They are remarkably life-like, they are sculptures of the real farmer who lives down the road and his real cows, who presumably couldn't be persuaded to stand in their picturesque positions for days on end. Look over the wall and you will find an even greater hoax: the farmer and his cows exist only from their torsos up. 'Well, it was just a bare wall until I put those sculptures there. I could have planted trees instead, but I'm not going to live long enough to see the trees grow big enough,' says Anita Roddick.

This garden is designed to be entertaining. It is also meant to be fun and to encourage activity. Hence Anita Roddick's ambition to have models of Fred Astaire and Ginger Rogers at the end of a path – to get

guests dancing. Hence the tennis court at the back of the garden with a small pavilion to one side kitted out with a little washing up place and a few other bits and pieces to make entertaining so far from the house a little easier; hence the yew bowling *allée* (very John Tradescant and Cranborne Manor this, except that this one has a fig-leafed figure playing bowls at the far end).

Contrasts and surprises, old and new mingle to make this garden. Crumbly old flint walls, typical of Sussex, are mixed with strong, sturdy, newly built, right-angled brick walls. There are marbled plinths dotted around the garden, one bearing a marbled apple core about four feet high. The explanation for this particular decoration is curious in itself: 'I've got the worst lighting ever in my garden. The lights are like the type you see in a caravan park and so I decided to cover them up with these Corinthian plinth things, and there was one in the orchard and so I thought, well, let's put a big chewed-up apple core on top of the plinth.' Anita Roddick talks so fast it is difficult to keep up with her.

Once she wanted a yellow brick road running through her garden to a pot of gold at the end of a rainbow. The yellow brick road has never materialized, but the rest of the project is up and running: the pot, a wonderful crock-like cauldron, is filled with 'gold' coins about six inches across. When I first visited this garden in 1986, a brightly coloured fibreglass rainbow tipped into the mouth of the pot. More recently that old rainbow has fallen from favour and been shoved into a rickety garden shed. This seemed a sad and improper end for a rainbow; its place has been taken by a spanking new, transparent perspex rainbow with subtle spatterings of each rainbow colour. 'The first rainbow was much too crude. The point of the rainbow, though, like many of the other things in the garden, is to keep the children, and everyone else, happy. A garden has got to be workable. When kids come with their parents the kids can play. I don't like these prissy gardens where you have to sit and look. There have to be places for kids to hide ... pots of gold so they can play rather than having to perambulate and admire with their parents.'

There is rosemary, rudbeckia, romneya, the beautiful papery tree poppy and the unusual *Berberis temolaica*. 'It is grown at Sissinghurst. It has a lovely pale leaf but unfortunately the blasted purple root stock keeps coming through,' says Julian Treyer-Evans, who is rightly proud of having got so much to grow on such thin topsoil over chalk. There is a shrub rose border which appears to be thriving, and the roses weren't even given special, extra-deeply dug-out areas in the chalk in which to spread their

THE CORE OF
THE GARDEN —
THIS COVERS
AN UNSIGHTLY
LIGHTING
INSTALLATION

119

roots. There is box edging and heather and *Euphorbia wulfenii* and mahonia and neat black bits of earth in between, and a trim lawn. The gardener cares a great deal about order and tidiness in the flower beds – there is no anarchy here. The anarchy is in the ideas.

'It's looking rather manicured at the moment. I hate it looking so manicured. I keep saying to the gardener, don't prune things, let things drip over a bit. I want to be able to make a garden which looks like a forty-year-old woman who is ripe and just about to burst and drop, and it does look like that in August, but in June, no. I like to be able to change the garden, I don't want it too manicured and static.'

Neat, round, almost Lutyens-style, brick-edged pools mixed in with stylized white-painted wooden palms stand a few yards from the tennis court. False palms and Lutyens seem to go together: Monkton House, Edward James's home, which is not so far away, has the same combination, although the whole of his house is Lutyens, real Lutyens, and the palms were larger and more realistically painted than those at Anita Roddick's garden.

A granite puck figure, his hair shooting up and back in a punk-like swirl, appears to be indicating something down the drive. And to one side of the yew *allée* there are two ponds, the higher, with a water spout in the shape of a frog, flowing into the lower. The water

THE BOWLING ALLÉE

FLYING GOLDFISH
AND THEIR WOODEN
PREDATORS

cascades from one to the other and activates three plastic goldfish on the end of wires. They dive back and forth as if they are jumping salmon-like from one pool to the next. 'There are some really good mistakes in this garden, and there are some tacky parts, like the pond with the permanently jumping fish. That was a great idea, but it just didn't work. The fish were too

heavy, the water coming through wasn't strong enough, so they have no tails and no heads because they have been broken off,' says Anita Roddick. 'I like form and balance with an element of chaos and surprise, and that's where the sculpture comes in.' There are many sculptures around the garden and she is planning more. She muses that perhaps the reason for

A FINAL FAREWELL FOR
THE MAN WHO THOUGHT THE RODDICK
GARDEN A BIT MUCH

this is because of some deep need within her to people the garden now that her children have grown up and left home.

Another enthusiasm which has grabbed her and may find its way into the garden is for poetry. She has always loved poetry, and she likes what Ian Hamilton Finlay has done with hard landscaping and poetry and puns in his remarkable garden at Stoneypath. Her next major project is on the horizon, metaphorically and literally: it is the conversion of the field beyond the garden horizon into a water garden. Not any old water garden, as you can imagine, but one with a series of ever larger pools, the last one appearing to almost melt in with the sky. And cascades, and alleys and ... unfortunately the Roddicks have decided that at the moment the project is a little too ambitious for them. But there is an interesting point about this field, one that lawn enthusiasts should bear in mind. The soil structure of the field is made up of six inches of topsoil over thick chalk but now, a few years after it was dug away, it is an attractive green sward, not as perfect as the text books would have it perhaps, but it is not intended to be. And it was encouraged without the help of mulches or fertilizers or weedkillers. In the first year after the field was dug away and then used as a dumping ground for chalk, the weeds took over. The field was rough-mown religiously until gradually, just like the text books say, the weed disappeared and the grasses took over. This pure, unfettered green makes a cool contrast to the riot of hard and soft landscaping in the main garden.

'At least it's not like a painting which you hide away for no one to see. This garden is for everyone to share. The garden is an expression of warmth. It is a brilliant party garden. There are barbecues every weekend in the summer and people arrive with lots of kids. It's just playtime. White parties are the traditional ones here, so people arrive in white, and there's white food to eat. It's wonderful. Like all our parties, tennis is played and croquet and there's great music. It's the sort of garden where everybody can just lounge around. It is a garden with a sense of humour. For those who are rich enough, the field next door is big enough to land helicopters in. I am not an isolationist. It's just the Italian in me, I guess. Like my mother. She always wants to feed everybody. You sit down for one plate of pasta and turn round and there's a second plate waiting for you.'

This abundance in spirit is reflected in the planting, which gives great sweeps of texture and colour to the garden. 'I love flowers but I can't stand those single daffodils under a tree which are an obsession with some English people. I love great swathes of flowers. I want five million of the little buggers coming down the hill rather than one nodding its little head. I've gone crazy over those little nodding tulips in the garden this spring. I told the gardener to take them out and replace them with a real, solid, courageous grouping of tulips. I get given lots because I do a lot of buying in Holland. It's colour and texture that fascinate me. I think one of the reasons the garden grows so well is the automatic watering system. It has increased the growing power of the garden so much. Sometimes I headbash the flowers if I think they're looking dull – like the lavender. I love lavender but we're having difficulty in making the lavender all nice and thick, so if they start getting too skimpy I'll just whip them out.'

ANITA RODDICK WITH TOAD
AND HER (NON-FIBREGLASS)
GARDENER IN THE BACKGROUND

WHEN GUESTS
LEAVE, THE
GARDEN STILL
HAS TO BE
PEOPLED

Despite this ruthlessness towards some plants, Anita Roddick can't bear to cut any of her garden flowers for the house, so instead she foots vast bills for cut flowers. Her desire for perfection in her garden means that the cost of manure and replacement plants comes to a considerable sum every year. That does not include the costs of any new garden project she puts into action: like the hornbeam alley planted very recently. The hornbeams were eight feet high when they were planted, and the trunks were bare up to the six-foot mark so the alley will look a little like French lime *allées*. And underneath the hornbeams there are African lilies, agapanthus.

There isn't a great deal of space for gardening in Anita Roddick's busy timetable, but whenever possible she likes to get out and weed, which is not odd when you consider that her family is Italian, and Italians are of course by tradition fine flower gardeners. 'My mother said that when I was forty I would start to love gardens. They provide a sense of continuity and they have a beginning, a middle and an end. It is my librium. Yesterday I was out there walking round it, playing in it, tidying it. I'm a great tidier. I live such a busy life that either it's librium or valium or dope or gin and tonic or cocaine and, as I don't want any of that, it's my garden which feeds my soul. That's why I don't give a toss about the cost: the garden gives me so much pleasure. And also I like to feel that I am doing something which is hard for people to destroy. If ever I leave the house, which I'm sure I won't, the garden is so lovely that I'm sure people will just want to keep it going.'

Riad El-Rayyes, another enthusiast who gives the impression, at least, that money is no object, hopes the same for his curious garden in a suburb of London. In 1987 he was chewing on one of his huge Havanas and wondering what to give his wife, Zeinat, for Christmas. What could he give the woman who is the mother of his two children, mistress of a splendid house, of two Persian cats called Liquorice and Toffee, of an African grey parrot called Bassem (after a journalist friend who happens to be a great talker) and of a large well-stocked conservatory spilling over with banana palms, citrus trees and exotics? What could he possibly give the woman who, it might seem to a casual onlooker, had everything?

What indeed? She loves gardens, so he felt that something for the garden might be appropriate. Then he hit on it: why bother with bits and pieces for the garden when he could give her a complete new garden. They had just moved into their Edwardian house, the builders had just moved out and so the plot they left behind had been churned and damaged any-way: drastic action was called for. What follows is a most outlandish story of the creation of a garden; for as any gardener knows, a garden evolves slowly, sometimes too slowly, so the magical appearance, practically overnight, of a beautiful garden, fully outfitted, seems worthy of mention.

It was just under three weeks until Christmas day, but Riad El-Rayyes, who is a publisher, art collector, and walking stick expert, went in search of a someone who loved taking on challenges and he found Mike Bayon, a local landscaper. As if by divine inspiration Riad El-Rayyes knew exactly what he wanted: the terrace outside his house should lead down to a bold plot bursting with colour and action; he wanted spec-tacular decoration and flowers and a garden his wife could enjoy and in which they could entertain their friends. He wanted a front garden overflowing with fruit as well as flowers and greenery. 'People asked me, but what if one apple or a pear should go, what if the fruit is stolen by passers by? But I said to them, who cares? Who wants the orchard pushed away at the back only?' And so, much against Mike Bayon's advice, cordon apple trees were planted. Now Mike Bayon admits he rather likes the effect, and indeed he has decided that many of his client's apparently bad ideas for the garden are extremely effective. Who

would have thought, for instance, that bright red and bright yellow roses clambering up the front of the house to twine their colours around the top windows would look anything but brash? In fact they look very fine and most attractive.

Riad El-Rayyes's ideas never stop coming, and as they come, so they have to be executed. He wants treasures bought from auctions, including his marble Buddhas and a few more besides to dot around the garden. Riad El-Rayyes likes Buddhas. There are other auction finds like a pair of stone Chinese dogs. Riad El-Rayyes likes dogs, too, though by their pro-portional number, not quite as much as Buddhas.

Above all else Riad El-Rayyes wants something really striking for his garden, something that will do more than mimic the stone urn respectability of so much hard landscaping, and so he decides it will be nice to plant a souvenir linked to his arrival in this country as a student thirty years ago: a telephone box, a proper old one, the type that has become a shrine for the Thirties Society and one or two caring individuals whose sturdy red phone boxes are lucky enough to have been saved from the current trend for yellow monsters.

'I used to sleep in one of these red telephone boxes at Liverpool Street station when I was a student at Cambridge.' What would the El-Rayyes family have

ABOVE THE
BUDDHA AND THE
BULLDOG, EAST
MEETS WEST

LEFT RIAD EL-
RAYYES AND TWO
SLIM BUDDHAS

made of this? Riad's father was a politician and journalist in Syria. He visited England just after the war, was seduced by the English garden, and so started a family interest in gardens which blossomed into the creation of one of the only English gardens in Damascus. The garden had everything, including spring bulbs in profusion which were imported specially from Holland. From this respectable background Riad came to England to find no room at any inn on his way up to Cambridge, merely a lowly red telephone box.

The telephone box had a smart new coat of paint, a back mirror and some glass shelves added. It now serves as a large drinks cabinet, generously supplied with soft drinks as well as alcohol to supply the needs of east and west and of ever more rigorous drinking-driving laws. Nearby a lavish barbecue area complete with a roof was added so that Riad El-Rayyes, a barbecue king of some note, could entertain his friends outside. All around the telephone box an appropriately English mixed border was planted. And behind that, well behind a hedge at the back of the garden, is an English orchard with apple trees and bluebells.

Then a post box had to be added because, well, Riad El-Rayyes likes the look of post boxes. A smart little freshly painted number was unearthed through an advertisement in the *Standard* and installed in the front garden. Then those about him pointed out that a front garden post box might well get a regular quota of letters. So the post box was moved to the back of the house, and turned into a wine cooler. Across the other side of the lawn a pond complete with a series of cascades was installed. It is one of those features which stubbornly refuses to work, leaving the plastic cascades sadly void of water – but the pond stays full. And now slugs, snails, frogs and tadpoles have started to cohabit with the goldfish which have regularly to be replaced. Augustus Finknottle, P. G. Wodehouse's noted newt fancier, would have loved this pond despite the fact that it lacks newts, because it is surrounded by stones and logs on which to sit and gaze into its depths.

As far as Riad El-Rayyes is concerned, one of the great advantages of plenty of hard landscaping is that his wife is more likely to go into the garden. She loves gardens but she doesn't care for mud, which is why she spends a lot of time in her conservatory with her parrot.

Next come the pigs. Riad El-Rayyes's dream has always been to move to the country and raise pigs, so in deference to this dream he has bought some little stone piglets. He likes owls too. Now that is truly contrary. In the west the owl stands for wisdom, but

ABOVE POST BOX EYE-CATCHER
POSING AS A WINE COOLER

LEFT RIAD EL-RAYYES'S MEMORIAL
TO HIS ARRIVAL IN THIS COUNTRY: A
TELEPHONE BOX, NOW A DRINKS
CABINET

RIGHT THERE WAS NO ROOM FOR
REAL PIGS IN RIAD EL-RAYYES'S
LONDON GARDEN

THIS TINY GARDEN INCLUDES A BUDDHA WALK

in his part of the world the owl represents pessimism. However, Riad's owls are the exception to the ruie. The house is alive with light and optimism, he smiles roundly and puffs while his daughter smiles and tickles the parrot's head and strokes the cat, and his wife beams too. Owls were dotted around the garden, and up one side of his terrace, in an impossibly small leg of land, a 'woodland and Buddha walk' was created with a few paving stones through the undergrowth. 'Please, please, cut me down to size,' he says, inviting criticism of his master plan. No one cuts him down to size.

No one doubted that his wife's Christmas present would be ready in time, or that Mike Bayon and his men would work long hours and all weathers with spotlights and canvas coverings to get it finished so that the El-Rayyes family could plan parties for thirty and forty of their friends throughout the summer. But for months after Christmas Riad El-Rayyes continued to employ the landscapers to add yet more to his landscape which proves the old adage: a gardener's work is never done.

Still, the Christmas garden was lovely, his wife adored it, and the Buddhas smiled.

MOST OF THIS GARDEN WAS
CREATED IN THREE WEEKS

Life and Death

Mellor's Garden, at Hough (pronounced huff) Hole House, is tucked into a narrow, steep-sided valley at the end of Sugar Lane in the village of Rainow, Cheshire. It is a remarkable garden, an allegory in two acres that tells the story of Christian's trials in John Bunyan's *The Pilgrim's Progress*. Uncle Tom's cabin makes a brief appearance, and so too does the tomb of James Mellor, son of a prosperous nineteenth-century cotton mill owner and the man who built this garden. To confuse things still further, the spiritual works of the eighteenth-century Swedish philosopher Emanuel Swedenborg have also helped shape this landscape.

Mellor was born in 1795 and died in 1891, and from the 1830s to the end of his life he devoted himself to creating his garden. He invited people to come and walk around the 'paths of life' on bank holidays and on Good Fridays, when he would lead them on their symbolic journey and then preach to them, reciting passages from the Bible and chunks of Swedenborg's philosophies.

Swedenborg's life had strong echoes for Mellor. Both came from religious fathers, both were interested in science and particularly astronomy. In 1745 Swedenborg, then an inventor and engineer, had a vision that persuaded him to give his life over to being a mystic and interpreter of religious works. He also came to believe that gardens were tremendously important in both a spiritual and a material sense. Swedenborg himself enjoyed a large garden with a maze, summer houses and a flower garden.

What better celebration of Mellor's deeply held religious beliefs and his respect for Swedenborg's philosophies than to build a physical representation of *The Pilgrim's Progress*?

James Mellor was brought up as a strict Methodist, and although he later rejected the Methodists his religious fervour never died. He was such a pious man that he invented an ingenious method of waking to the sound of hymns: he had a wooden handle beside his bed that controlled an automatic organ powered by a waterwheel in a cave beneath the house. His father James Mellor moved him and the rest of the family to Hough Hole House before James was one year old, so that the family could oversee the building of a cotton mill just down the road.

After many years of neglect, Mellor's garden has now been restored by the current owners, Mr and Mrs Gordon Humphreys. They bought Hough Hole House in 1978, after moving from London. Gordon Humphreys wanted to go back to his original work as

THE WICKET GATE, THE START OF
CHRISTIAN'S JOURNEY, AT MELLOR'S
GARDEN NEAR MACCLESFIELD

an engineer, and he wanted to return to the area where he was born. They stumbled on Hough Hole House ten days before it was due to be auctioned. They bought it in the knowledge that they already had a connection with the house: this was the place where Gordon had been taught for a few months while he was a tiny child, having been evacuated during the war from Manchester. The portents were right, and so was the house, so they bought it without knowing anything about Mellor's Garden. In 1983 some conservationists came to inspect the area and discovered the heritage treasure buried beneath the Victorian beds, overgrown paths and silted ponds.

The Humphreys might have thought they had bought an ordinary property; instead they had bought an (albeit overgrown) institution, one that would soak up their time and energy and cause them to dress up in seventeenth-century Puritans' outfits on certain Christian feast days. With the help of the local conservationist and historian, Richard Turner, they turned up original sources, they spoke to local people and even found pictures of the original garden. It was a mammoth task, because so little appeared to be left under the late nineteenth-century planting and the undergrowth that choked the paths and some of the pond. Some might have been tempted to call in the bulldozers. The Humphreys set to work themselves to clear and restore the garden to its former glory.

Originally every tree planted in the garden was a variety mentioned in the Bible, from the tree of heaven to the yew. The Miss Russells who bought the house from the Mellor family in 1927 and who taught Gordon Humphreys, planted rhododendrons, and the Humphreys decided to show mercy to these Himalayan plants although they weren't in keeping with the rest of the garden. The small huts and pavilions around the garden were restored. And then a local man in his eighties arrived on the doorstep with a confession: as a naughty schoolboy he and his school friends had climbed into the garden and toppled a large statue of a fish into the pond. He had no idea if it was still there, or whether or not it was broken. So the Humphreys cleared the area of the hill's spring-fed lake indicated by the villager. A foot down – nothing. Two feet, still nothing, three feet, nothing. Four feet down a fish tail could just be seen. They tied a rope around it and gently pulled as the running water washed away the mud and dirt. It was an ornate fish balancing on its fairly menacing mouth. They realized that this was Apollyon, one of Christian's trials, the terrifying bear-fish-lion monster. All that was missing from the newly dredged-up Apollyon were the lion's paws which were mentioned in Bunyan's description of the beast.

STAIRS
REPRESENTING
MOUNT SINAI
LEAD UP TO
THE HOWLING
HOUSE, WHERE
SULPHUROUS
STENCHES AND
WILD SCREAMS
GREET
PILGRIMS

LEFT A REVOLVING
SUMMERHOUSE, THE HOLY
SEPULCHRE

ABOVE ONE OF THE MANY
TABLETS CARVED BY JAMES
MELLOR WITH HIS SAYINGS

Eccentric Gardens

Elsewhere, in their search through old store rooms, one or two strange little free-standing 'windows' came to light, after years of being forgotten and left to gather dust. These were framed and glazed pieces of printed paper on which Mellor had set out his religious and philosophical thoughts and musings. Mellor used to dot the windows around the garden to be read as the pilgrims followed the path, although sadly there is no record of which window went where, so they live in 'Heaven', which seems only right.

The more the Humphreys dug, in their garden and in the archives, the more they found, and the more people came forward with bits and pieces pertinent to Swedenborg, Mellor and the garden. One old lady turned up a lead printing block she had been using as a teapot stand: it was an ornately decorated printing block of a page setting out Swedenborg's rules of life:

I   To read often and to meditate well on the Word of God.
II To be always resigned and content under the Dispensations of Providence.
III Always to observe a Propriety of Behaviour, and to preserve the Conscience clear and void of offence.
IV To obey that which is ordained; to be faithful in the discharge of duties of our employment; and to do everything in our power to render ourselves as universally useful as possible.

Today it is possible for the devout and the curious to tread the pilgrim's path as it was experienced in much of the last century. The pilgrimage begins along any of the paths that leads to the garden from the outside world. No matter who you are or from where you have travelled, the path you choose is considered to have led from the City of Destruction. Just outside the garden, the pilgrim encounters the Slough of Despond, now, disappointingly, a small car park at the front of the Humphreys' house. Here you just have to imagine the oozing marsh of the last century. The journey proper begins at the Wicket Gate, exactly that, to one side of the house. Christian is directed there by the Evangelist and warned to keep on the straight and narrow, which, as a visitor soon sees, is not always the easiest path to take. It winds round the side of the house to the back where the old stable block once was. Now it is a garage, but for the purposes of the Holy Way this is the House of the Interpreter, where Christian is shown the face of Christ.

The next stops are the Cross – now only a stone pillar remains, the rest having been broken off – and the Holy Sepulchre, which is Mellor's round summer house. The Humphreys have restored it and placed it on a revolving plinth, which was a common feature of nineteenth-century summer houses. Up the path we go along slippery slabs set on a remarkably steep slope. This is the Hill Difficulty (appropriately, it was completely overgrown with stinging nettles when the

THE HILL OF DIFFICULTY

lions looked frightfully fierce. These more resemble stately cats, and they came with the Humphreys from their last house. Across the river from the lions comes the really confusing part of the journey, because suddenly we jump several continents and a century or so to be swept into the episode from *Uncle Tom's Cabin* in which Eliza the slave girl escapes from her wicked master across an ice-covered river on the point of thawing. The river politely breaks up after Eliza has run across and her pursuers cannot follow. She finds safety at Uncle Tom's cabin, a small stone hut which doubles as the Lodge to the Palace Beautiful in *Pilgrim's Progress*. The ice is represented by a vast slab of stone balanced between the two banks of a stream. It wobbles convincingly as it is crossed.

At this point a small path edges along the side of the Pool of Siloam (the large and tranquil garden pond) decorated with gargoyles from derelict churches which were picked up by Mrs Humphreys' father, who was a clergyman. This is the Valley of Humiliation, where Christian meets Apollyon the foul monster '... clothed with scales like a fish, he had wings like a dragon, feet like a bear and out of his belly came fire and smoke, and his mouth was as the mouth of a lion.' The Apollyon in Mellor's Garden looks a much more cheery creature – a stylized fishy statue with his tail curled heavenwards. And the small, dusty niche in

Humphreys arrived). The view from the top is of Mr and Mrs Humphreys' house, once Mellor's home ... the Palace Beautiful.

Down the other side of the hill we pass two charming stone lions guarding the walk. They are meant to be one of Christian's trials. Perhaps Mellor's original

FROM THE HILL
OF DIFFICULTY THE
PILGRIMS LOOKED DOWN
TO THE PALACE
BEAUTIFUL, JAMES MELLOR'S
HOUSE. TODAY
IS HOME TO THE
HUMPHREYS' FAMILY

the bank at the end of the Valley of the Shadow of Death doesn't appear very scary either, although it represents the mouth of Hell.

The Holy Way continues to Vanity Fair, a pretty planted area just at the back of the house. It was overgrown when the Humphreys arrived so they cleared the area and planted it with juniper, bluebells, ferns, primulas and lilies-of-the-valley. And when recently an old lady walked around the garden for the first time since she was a girl, she said how nice it was to see that the same old lilies-of-the-valley were still flourishing! On the other side of the path there is the Plain of Ease, a grassy bank planted with Jacob's ladder, and then comes the Hill Lucre. Nearby stands Lot's wife, a great pillar of stone with one hole at the top, eyeing the surrounding hills with hollow menace, and finally comes the meadow by the River of God, bathed in sun, beside the splashing millstream which is fed by the pond. Up the side of the valley again and at the top the ground opens out into a flat mown field. This was Mellor's tennis court. It is also By Path Meadow where Christian sleeps. Vain-confidence, however, falls into the ditch to one side, and dies.

From the meadow you can see the chimneys of a nearby building, Hough Hole farmhouse, which Mellor owned and so felt able to make it his Doubting Castle, where wicked Giant Despair locked Christian in the dungeons. The pilgrims escape after much nastiness and head for the Holy Way and the Delectable Mountains. The 'mountains' are represented by a marvellous stone seat set into the hillside. Two great stone flags make the seat. It was a winter day when I sat there for a moment and yet, despite the cold, this solid stone structure was one of the most comfortable garden benches I've ever tried. Very appropriate, because this is where the pilgrims rest and revive themselves, although Bunyan describes the area as being dotted with vines and fountains of water, which are difficult to arrange in this valley outside Macclesfield. From there they wend their way along Mount Error to the By Way to Hell.

Mellor wanted to give his pilgrims some hell fire to remember, so to create the stench of brimstone and the wild screaming effects which might be imagined to be truly hellish, he built a small and rather pretty stone hut with a grate and a tiny window cut into the back of the room opposite the entrance. Before visitors were taken round the garden, the fire in the hut would be stoked up and sulphur added, and an aeolian harp placed in the back window, so that as Mellor opened the door a reek of brimstone would greet his guests, followed by terrible cries made by the wind passing through the strings of the harp.

THE WOBBLY
BRIDGE
LEADING TO
UNCLE TOM'S
CABIN, OR THE
LODGE TO THE
PALACE
BEAUTIFUL,
DEPENDING ON
WHICH STORY
YOU ARE
FOLLOWING AT
THE TIME

Life and Death

THIS ELEGANT FISH MONSTER REPRESENTS APOLLYON

Eccentric Gardens

The original harp had disappeared, so Mrs Humphreys decided to make a replacement. She looked 'aeolian harp' up in *Encyclopaedia Britannica*, bought pine, mahogany and cat-gut, and made the box-like instrument as a surprise for her husband. It didn't work. But then, one Good Friday with a fine westerly blowing, she took some visitors up to the 'Howling House' and, just as she was about to explain that it didn't work, a dreadful howling and screaming began.

We step over some low iron railings in the Country of Beulah, signified by the three magnificent Mellor family tombstones, one of them Mellor's own, which he himself designed before his death.

WHEN I CAN NO LONGER SPEAK
LET THIS STONE SPEAK FOR ME
AND SAY, LIVE NEAR TO GOD,
CAREFULLY HEAR HIS WORD, AND THE
WRITINGS OF SWEDENBORG, YOU WILL
SEE THEIR HARMONY.
LIVE ACCORDINGLY AND YOU WILL
BEHOLD WONDERFUL THINGS

The Dark River, beyond the tombstones, isn't very dark and it isn't a river: it is a slit of a path running down from the Country of Beulah to the Slough of Despond. We cross it to come close to our goal: the Celestial City on Mount Sion. Mount Sion is an elegant stone and iron spiral staircase up to Mellor's small whitewashed chapel-cum-observatory, the Celestial City, with an inscription above the door which reads 'With all thy getting, get understanding 1844.' Depending on whether the building was being treated as his observatory or heaven, Mellor would whip his telescope away in a back cupboard.

Outside this building as many as five hundred people would gather together on a Good Friday to listen to Mellor's preachings after a guided tour around the garden. Today the Humphreys guide without preaching, leaving individuals to draw their own conclusions. 'People seem to like to rest awhile in the Celestial City. Sometimes they pray, sometimes they just sit here. People seem to like the atmosphere', says Mrs Humphreys.

Mellor's Garden is, probably, the only garden in England which tells a story contained in a book as well as expounding a philosophy. Imagine the mental problems of having to maintain such a garden. It is a good thing the Humphreys are calm, level-headed people or they might be unnerved by living so close to heaven and hell, and having a Holy Sepulchre for a summer house. Sometimes a demanding hellebore or some tiresome flowering shrubs make it horticulturally necessary to take the evil path rather than the straight and narrow. Sometimes the good path has to be ignored simply in order to trim the edges of flower beds or of the paths themselves, to replace a

Eccentric Gardens

flagstone which has started to ease its way down the hill or to trim a yew tree. But in taking such a path, can the sinner gardener ignore the symbolism? Mr and Mrs Humphreys do, and without them the garden would probably still be forgotten, a wilderness linked to a few funny old wives' tales from the village about a religious garden which once existed.

It is wholly appropriate that a temporal representation of the celestial city, or paradise, should have been built in a garden, because the word paradise is derived from the old Persian word 'pairidaeza' which means 'an enclosure' or 'a walled garden'. In eastern and western cultures, in Islam, Christianity and in many more ancient religions and civilizations, the garden is often seen as synonymous with paradise, heaven and the finding of bliss, and the making of a garden is often a metaphor for the earthly route to the finding of paradise.

In the south of England there is another garden which illustrates the journey of life, and of man's struggle between heaven and hell, this one far more personal than that at Mellor's garden. This is a garden where one man, John Comino-James, has set out his autobiography in concrete. Images of his path through life are laid out in sculptural pavements around his garden in Oxfordshire. At first glance all

the paving sculptures appear to be mazes or labyrinths, and indeed most are in one form or another, although more complicated than most. These are serious mazes, art forms rather than entertainment, although John Comino-James has no objection to those who want to regard his mazes as entertainment.

In 1984 John Comino-James 'acknowledged an urgent ambition to construct a large maze', and he has never looked back. His once-conventional two-acre garden is now a journey through an autobiography. Having found the art form with which he wanted to express his forty-five years, he had then to decide what kind of maze it should be. For instance, should it be a frivolous maze with dead ends and only one true path to the centre, or should it be a path that led from A to B? Not directly from A to B but a meander, wherein the path would wind and switch back in just the way that life's fortunes and misfortunes weave about in the most unpredictable fashion. He decided on the latter type of maze. In other words, the maze would be unicursal – it would have no false turnings, blind alleys or alternative routes. The multicursal maze at Hampton Court, which is very popular, is the other sort. Then came the choice of whether it should be constructed of spiral or concentric circles, and how many segments would it have? How many loops

JOHN COMINO-JAMES AND A PEBBLE OUTLINE
OF ONE OF HIS AUTOBIOGRAPHICAL SCULPTURES

should it involve and how like one of the old English turf mazes, those ancient labyrinths whose function still isn't clear?

There were so many forms from which to choose, and although John Comino-James knew that his immediate goal was a large unicursal maze, he found that he had first to construct some smaller pavement mazes or sculptures. Indeed, the more he tried to decide exactly how the large maze should be designed, the more dead ends he came to, and instead of being able to proceed with his original plan he found himself involved in a series of diversionary constructions, the first of these being the octagonal pavement maze to one side of his rectangular home. This maze has vague echoes of the three-sided bay windows of the house. It is unicursal, and it is a design inspired by some lines written by T. S. Eliot:

We shall not cease from explorations
And the end of our exploring
Will be able to arrive where we started
And know the place for the first time.

Then came the S-shaped double spiral, an elegant double curl of Celtic-looking paving set to one side of the yard; then a pattern of a ladder set into a paved terrace bordered by Portuguese laurel, overhung by elder and willow, which leads to The Wheel: two concentric circles that surround and dissect a complex web of meticulously cut concrete paving. 'There are twenty-four segments in the larger circles, and seventy (or three score and ten) in the smaller, one's day slightly out of centre with one's life, that perpetual tension,' says John Comino-James and amplifies the idea with a quotation from W. H. Auden's 'In memory of W. B. Yeats':

In the deserts of the heart
Let the healing fountain start
In the prison of his days
Teach the free man how to praise.

One path – or pavement sculpture – in his garden ends in a coil reminiscent of a spiral shell. As we stand there he recites a poem by e. e. cummings:

Seeker of truth.
Follow no path
All paths lead where
Truth is here

The next sculpture we come to is an odd looking pattern of paving and bricks which Comino-James explains as 'an explosion of fragments escaping from a restraining circle'. It depends how you look at it, because it could be seen to be fragments of paving/ life/whatever pushing their way back into the security of a circle.

Finally there is the main maze, the structure he set out to make in the first place. It is in the back garden surrounded by the beginnings of a yew hedge which

T. S. ELIOT
INSPIRED THIS
IMAGE

151

A SNAKE IN THE GRASS,
COMINO-JAMES'S
S-SHAPED DOUBLE SPIRAL

will one day circle the whole of this circular maze. Although it seems like cheating, it is tempting to walk across to the centre by the direct route but Comino-James makes it clear that the proper path must be experienced, that the maze must be trodden. We set off briskly, tracing out John Comino-James's life along the paviours. 'The idea of life as a journey is both axiomatic and fascinating to me, and the labyrinth is an emblem of that journey on both the physical and spiritual planes.' Suddenly from the outside of the circle I am within one small hop of the centre, but hardly am I there before the path throws itself, and me, to the outside again. It's no use trying to guess where the path will throw one next – the thin

THIS SPIRAL SHELL PAVEMENT
SCULPTURE WAS INSPIRED
BY E. E. CUMMINGS

white lines of paving in the turf mingle into each other in a dizzy-making way as one treads one's way around the maze. There are echoes here of Archbishop Runcie's dreams: 'I had a dream of a maze,' he said in his enthronement address. 'There were some people very close to the centre but they could not find a way through. Just outside the maze, others were standing.

They were further away from the heart of the maze, but they would be there sooner than the party that fretted and fumed inside.'

We arrive at the centre. I stand there triumphant, even though it is not through any of my own skill that I have arrived. John Comino-James says in a shocked voice that he has never come across anyone doing the

maze so fast – or standing on the actual centre piece. But then, he muses, the approach and treatment of a maze by the pilgrim is significant and interesting in itself.

That is the point about all the structures he has created. For him they are an expression of personal fascinations and concerns, but for others they will have different meanings or perhaps no meaning at all, beyond being an object of entertainment. John Comino-James is keen to spread the idea that a maze can be anybody's and that any kind of garden decoration – or indeed art in general – can be anybody's, no matter how rich or poor the creator. Here speaks the man who once studied and photographed traffic flow on the A412 at Denham in the name of art. John Comino-James rails at those who seek Truth or Art by visiting only such famous sites as the Acropolis or Palladio's Villa Rotunda.

The garden is both interesting and attractive, although not everyone thinks so: one of those who told me about John Comino-James's garden said in awed tones, 'Well, I wouldn't bother with it if I were you: the garden's *awful* – such a mess. The man doesn't like plants and so he simply concretes over everything.' Which is completely untrue, because although Comino-James doesn't go for the flower garden or cottage garden style, he has planted beech,

yew and laurel hedges and a spinney of woodland trees to complement his peculiar structures. In such a setting he creates his mazes so that they look from a distance as if they are simple, elegant designs of brick laid into the turf around the chapel-like house that is his home.

When he and his wife and their two daughters moved here – from a bungalow without much outdoor space – friends and relations arrived bearing gifts of rhododendrons, unusual shrubs, pretty plants and newly sown seedlings . . . most of which went the way of the flesh rather more quickly than their donors had expected. Comino-James, beard flowing in the wind, would accept them and then forget about them as he paced his garden and his soul trying to bring light from one to the other.

Like so many of us Comino-James felt his life to be in a tangle, but unlike the rest of us who pretend it isn't really, and who plough on regardless, scared to look at the tangle for fear it will all seem too terrible on closer examination, John Comino-James wanted to examine and explore his tangles. He carries guilt about having access to an enviable fortune, not only in material wealth but in terms of more general good fortune: his health, his family and his friends. He is gentle and bohemian, and he worries terribly, a trait that sits strangely with his wild, woolly appearance. Perhaps

there is a certain therapeutic value for him both in designing these pavements and mazes, and in then actually doing most of the manual work himself, although he is anxious to acknowledge help from his loyal and increasingly intrigued assistant Jos Palanca. When Comino-James talks about the physical side of his works it is more than the actual physical following of the path; it is clear that he has also enjoyed the physical construction: 'I've really loved having my own concrete mixer. Everybody should have one.'

Mazes can be made of anything: water, brick, wood – or even chess pieces, in the case of one in a California hotel where the sixteen-foot-high hedges are topped with topiary kings, queens, knights and pawns. But Comino-James feels strongly that a lack of the means to afford swish materials and fabrics should not bar anyone from creativity: art is all about us in both meanings of the phrase, and so it should be inclusive, not exclusive.

Search back to the first recorded mazes and they too were made by people who had access only to simple construction materials. The earliest known British mazes are two carvings found near the craggy coast normally associated with the legend of King Arthur, Tintagel in Cornwall. The carvings, seven Cretan rings, were unearthed in 1942, but date from between 1400 and 1800 BC. The more common ancient mazes

Stan Clark Esq.
4 Box Lanes
Minchinhampton
Stroud
GL6 9DH
Tel Brimscombe 0453 884004

Chapter Five
OXFORDSHIRE
Robert Heber Percy and Lord Berners' garden, immortalized in Nancy Mitford's *The Pursuit of Love*, and now owned by Sofka Zinovieff is open on one day during the spring through the National Gardens Scheme. Quite apart from the eccentricities, this garden is well worth a visit: the planting and the landscaping are very beautiful.
Faringdon House
Faringdon
SN7
The folly, just outside Faringdon proper, is open on the first Sunday of every month in summer.

BUCKINGHAMSHIRE
West Wycombe Park, a magnificent eighteenth century landscape which includes the erotic Venus garden is open through the National Trust.
West Wycombe Park
Nr High Wycombe
HP14 3HA
For times and ticket prices consult the National Trust or contact 0494 24411

Chapter Six
HUMBERSIDE
The plastic parrot and Swiss chalet garden behind Hull City football ground. A garden of innovation and love where the colourful garden ornament is allowed outdoors only during the summer when it can't be hurt by frost and foul weather. Write to make an appointment to see the garden.
Mr and Mrs Fred Button
38 Sledmere Grove
Hull
HU4 6LD

NORTHUMBERLAND
The cement menagerie of concrete animals and real and story book people is open during daylight hours every day of the year. Teas are sometimes served during summer. There is a collection box at the gate, and every penny is needed to keep this magnificent, privately run garden going.
For details contact
John Fairnington Esq.
The Fountain Garden
Branxton
Cornhill on Tweed
TD12 4SW
Tel 089 082 211

SUSSEX
West Dean Gardens which include the horses' teeth floor (for opening details see Chapter 1).

AVON
Banwell Bone Garden, Caves and Victorian 'Druid's Temple'. The two couples who own this garden, the Haynes and the Sargeants will open their gardens by appointment. They are in desperate need of funds to continue restoration work and to replant the garden. Donations are gratefully received.
Yvonne and Ronald Sargeant and Margaret and John Haynes
The Caves
Banwell
Nr Weston Super Mare
BS24 6NA
Tel 0934 820516

Chapter Seven
SUSSEX
Anita Roddick's party garden. Never open to the public.

LONDON
Riad N El-Rayyes' party garden. Never open to the public.

Chapter Eight
CHESHIRE
Mellor's garden, the work of a devoutly religious nineteenth century mill owner who created an allegorical garden based on the story of Bunyan's *Pilgrim's Progress*. It has been lovingly and accurately restored by the current owners of the house and garden, the Humphreys. Visitors by appointment only, contact:
Mrs Humphreys
Sugar Lane
Rainow
Nr Macclesfield
SK10 5UW
Tel 0625 72286

OXFORDSHIRE
Maze or labyrinth garden. A garden of paving sculptures which tell the story of the owner's life and struggles. Allow plenty of time to see this garden.
The creator, owner, John Comino-James, will allow visitors by appointment only.
Write to:
Shepherds Close
Kingston Stert
Chinnor
OX9 4NL

Gardens of England and Wales, the National Gardens Scheme 'Yellow Book' which lists private gardens open to the public is available at book shops and garden centres and some gardens, or directly from the National Gardens Scheme Charitable Trust, Hatchlands Park, East Clandon, Guildford, Surrey GU4 7RT, Tel 0483 211535

Acknowledgements

My husband Johnnie Keyes, my accomplice on manic garden tours through sun, wind and rain; my parents, Gaie and Toby, for inspiring in me their love of gardens and for helping me write this book; to Jean Laughton who broke off her retirement from the BBC to help me with some background research to this book; Dr Brent Elliott the RHS librarian; the National Gardens Scheme central and county organizers; to Mark Hailes whose computer whizzkiddery rescued me and the book from being sucked into a new technology black hole; to the National Trust, both Warren Davies in the head office and many of the regional area organizers; to the Royal Botanic Gardens, Kew; Hugh Palmer; Oliver Gillie; Peter Hayden; Andrew Best; Jillie Speed; Adam Peters and, most important of all, the garden owners who kindly agreed to be included in this book.